Colonial Bureaucrats and the Mexican Economy

American University Studies

Series IX
History
Vol. 13

PETER LANG
New York · Berne · Frankfurt am Main

John S. Leiby

Colonial Bureaucrats and the Mexican Economy

Growth of a Patrimonial State, 1763 - 1821

PETER LANG
New York · Berne · Frankfurt am Main

Library of Congress Cataloging-in-Publication Data

Leiby, John S.
Colonial bureaucrats and the Mexican economy : growth of a patrimonial state, 1763-1821.

(American university studies. Series IX, History ; vol. 13)
Bibliography: p.
1. Mexico—Economic policy. 2. Bureaucracy—Mexico—History. 3. Mexico—History—Spanish Colony, 1540-1810. I. Title II. Series.
HC134.L35 1986 338.972 86-7369
ISBN 0-8204-0239-7

CIP-Kurztitelaufnahme der Deutschen Bibliothek

Leiby, John S.:
Colonial Bureaucrats and the Mexican Economy : Growth of a Patrimonial State, 1763 - 1821 / John S. Leiby. - New York ; Berne ; Frankfurt am Main : Lang, 1986.
(American University Studies : Ser. 9, History ; Vol. 13)
ISBN 0-8204-0239-7
NE: American University Studies / 09

Printed by Weihert-Druck GmbH, Darmstadt (West-Germany)

TO MY PARENTS,

JUDY & AUSTIN LEIBY

TABLE OF CONTENTS

PREFACE

Over the last quarter century, the history of colonial Spanish America has remained an active field of research and scholarship. Historians consequently have led the way in reconstructing this vibrant yet fragmentary history of "Spain in America." At the beginning of the twentieth century only a few scholars chose to explore the meaning and influence of the Spaniards in the New World. Both Herbert Bolton and Edward Bourne were among the first to redirect the American historical community toward the Spanish influence in the Western Hemisphere. Since then, Latin American history, including the frontier regions, have grown into a field with its own identity. Nonetheless Latin American history has tended to be written and researched on the basis of success or failure. The Bourbon reforms, for instance, were neither a total success nor a total failure. Bourbon Mexico, which the succeeding pages convey, was a complex society and the policies adopted in the late eighteenth century were complex as well. This present study is therefore neither the story of success or failure but rather somewhere between these two extremes. It is a saga of people and how they tried mold their society into a modernized entity. Both politics and economics played an integral role in the development of late Bourbon Mexico. While officials in Spain drafted ordinances and decrees, colonial bureaucrats implemented and modified policies which would fit into the colonial setting.

Controversy exists within the historical community as to the actual meaning of the Bourbon reforms and their impact upon Spanish America. By the late eighteenth century and the advent of the Caroline reforms the structure of colonial politics had taken a decided advance--an advance toward patrimonialism. This new state is most apparent in Bourbon Mexico with regard to the administration of the economy. Indeed, the Spanish Bourbons reformed the bureaucracy of late colonial Mexico with their sights on the possible economic gains which might be achieved and thus add power to the patrimonial state. Efficiency and economic prosperity thereby became the primary objectives of colonial bureaucrats and the Spanish crown.

This present study is consequently an analysis of the economy of late Bourbon Mexico and how the colonial bureaucrats tried to promote the expansion of the economy. Policy changes were offered by viceroys, intendants, merchants, and economists to spur economic development. In reality, the patrimonial state helped to create a semi-planned economy in late colonial Mexico. Late Bourbon Mexico was patrimonial in the sense that the Bourbon monarchs considered New Spain as an inherited patrimony and its subjects children of the Spanish Empire. The colonial bureaucrats of late colonial Mexico were primarily Spanish in ethnic composition and therefore adopted policies which were beneficial chiefly to the Spanish crown and Spaniards serving in the late Mexican colony. New Spain was a highly stratified society and Mexicans seldom rose in social rank. The Bourbon reformers transformed the Mexican colony into a society which served the mothercountry--Spain. Late colonial Mexico consequently was a patrimonial state and society--administered for the benefit of the Bourbon monarchs and Spaniards serving there.

The revival of the Mexican economy during the late eighteenth century undoubtedly benefited the entire colony. Economic rewards, however, were distributed according to social class. The greatest rewards went to the Spanish and creole elements while far less went to the castes and Indians of New Spain. Thus the economy of late Bourbon Mexico was patrimonial both in its administration and operation.

This monograph is divided into two distinct parts. The first outlines the economic structure of late colonial Mexico and how this diversified economy fared under the aegis of colonial bureaucrats and Caroline reforms. By the late eighteenth century, bureaucrats were not merely observers but rather were advisers and actually implemented economic policies with varying degrees of success. The second part is concerned with the patrimonial state and how it influenced the social and economic history of late Bourbon Mexico.

Bureaucrats were essential to the smooth running of the Spanish Empire. Many, especially during the late colonial period, were well trained and educated. Almost every daily pursuit in late Bourbon Mexico was affected by the bureaucracy and consequently by the patrimonial state. It was the bureaucrats who informed the Bourbon monarchs about colonial conditions and influenced the direction of colonial policies. Without efficient and dedicated bureaucrats the Spanish Empire would not have persevered as long as it did. Indeed, it was this cadre plus the colonial elites who upheld and promoted the patrimonial state.

This study is based principally upon primary materials gathered in Spain and Mexico. In Sevilla the Archivo General de Indias remains an essential source for any scholar studying Mexico's colonial heritage. In Madrid the major repositories of colonial Spanish manuscripts are the Museo Naval, Real Academía de la Historía, Biblioteca Nacional, Biblioteca Central Militar, and Biblioteca del Palacio Real. In Mexico two archives are noteworthy: the Archivo General de la Nación and Archivo Histórico de Hacienda. In writing this study I have drawn heavily and liberally from the sources in these institutions.

This monograph is the product of some six years of research and writing. As with all scholars I owe a number of professional debts. Foremost I must acknowledge my parents who put up with me for so many years--listening to my ideas as well as my rantings. Others who provided valuable advice and encouragement include Noel J. Stowe of Arizona State University, Lewis A. Tambs, U.S. Ambassador to Costa Rica, Thomas L. Karnes, the former History Department Chairman at Arizona State University, Diego Rivero of the Bibliotheca Americana and University of Miami, Horst Pietschmann of the University of Cologne, West Germany, Charles C. Colley of the University of Texas at Arlington, Manuel P. Servín, formerly of Arizona State University and the University of New Mexico, David K. Strate, L.G. Moses, Katharine F. Nutt, and Delno C. West, all of Northern Arizona University, Salvador Reynoso of the Universidad Autónoma de Guadalajara, Mexico, Emilio Leal del Valle of Madrid, Spain, and finally Don Armando Represa, Director of the Archivo General de Simancas. Any errors, whether historical or stylistic, are mine alone. Finally, I must acknowledge the patience and encouragement of Jay Wilson, Editor-in-Chief of Peter Lang Publishing, Incorporated. Without the support of the people listed above this work would never have been completed.

John S. Leiby
November 1985

ARCHIVAL ABBREVIATIONS

AGI	Archivo General de Indias, Sevilla
AGN	Archivo General de la Nación, Mexico City
AHH	Archivo Histórico de Hacienda, Mexico City
AHN	Archivo Histórico Nacional, Madrid
BL	Biblioteca Central Militar, Madrid
BL	Bancroft Library, Berkeley, California
BM	British Museum, London
BMEX	Biblioteca Nacional de México, Mexico City
BPR	Biblioteca del Palacio Real, Madrid
CECDNS	Arizona State University, Tempe, Arizona; Charles Trumbull Hayden Memorial Library, Collection of Eighteenth Century Documents of New Spain, Microfilm Collections
HNM	Hemeroteca Nacional de México, Mexico City
LC	Library of Congress, Washington, D.C.
MN	Museo Naval, Madrid
RAH	Real Academía de la Historía, Madrid

LIST OF TABLES

LIST OF ILLUSTRATIONS

CHAPTER I

EIGHTEENTH CENTURY SPANISH ECONOMISTS AND THEIR INFLUENCE UPON BOURBON REFORMS

Spanish commerce with the Indies declined markedly in the seventeenth century as the result of Hapsburg policy and the disastrous effects of the Thirty Years War. José de Veitia Linaje reported in 1672 that transatlantic trade had declined to such an extent that it was a miracle any ships arrived in the Indies.[1] Hapsburg commercial policies restricted trade with the Indies for the benefit of the metropolis. Trade with the Indies was exclusively controlled by the _Casa de Contratación_ (Board of Trade) and the consulado (merchants' guild), both based in Sevilla. The _Casa_ regulated trade by limiting the ports through which trade goods could be shipped or received. The consulado constrained commerce by limiting trading privileges to members of the consulado and by restricting trade goods to those which brought a high rate of return.[2] It was in response to the decline of Spanish transatlantic commerce that the Bourbon dynasty initiated a century-long program to revive trade with the empire.

The entrance of the Bourbons into Spain in the early eighteenth century greatly changed Spanish economic thought and policies. Philip V, first Bourbon monarch of Spain, realized the need for economic reform and initiated the first of the commercial reforms. As a partial solution to Spain's commercial decline, he ordered the transfer of the Casa de Contratación in 1717 to the port of Cádiz, thus diffusing the economic influence of the Sevilla consulado. Registration of goods and release by crown officials for further sale and purchase now took place at the port of Cádiz. In April 1720, as part of the program of commercial reform, the king ordered a complete renovation of the flotas (fleet or convoy) system. The principal feature of this plan was a precise time schedule for ships trading with the Indies. The plan, however, ended in failure. Ships traveling to the Indies continued to leave on an irregular basis.[3]

Although the Bourbons are noted for their reforming spirit, they utilized or integrated in their commercial reform schemes many efficient Hapsburg institutions. Initially, the Junta de Comercio established under the Hapsburgs in 1679 had total power in questions involving trade. The Bourbons altered this institution during the early years of the eighteenth century. They added the areas of mining, manufacturing, and minting to the jurisdiction of this committee. Along with these administrative changes, the Bourbons renamed the committee in 1730. The new title was Junta de Comercio y Moneda. This committee remained the principal body which advised the king on economic matters until the 1787 establishment of the Junta del Estado made it the dominant policy-making body in Spain.[4]

During the course of the eighteenth century, the crown and its ministers began to pay closer attention to the suggestions of economists for economic and commercial reform. As the century progressed, Spain's economic theorists became increasingly influenced by French economic theory. Most eighteenth century Spanish economists were critical of traditional imperial restrictions which retarded Spanish colonial administration and economic activity. In essence, these enlightened Spanish economists advocated a compromise between laissez-faire and mercantilism.[5]

The premier Spanish economist of the early eighteenth century was Jerónimo de Uztaríz. Born in Santisteban, sometime in the last third of the seventeenth century, Uztaríz died between 1730 and 1742. In 1724, he published his most important treatise, _Teórica y práctica de comercio y marina_. In this work he primarily condemned the excessive duties which remained in the structure of trade, insisting that they hastened the decline of economic development in Spain. He maintained that Spain's normal colonial trade had been replaced by a thriving contraband trade. Uztaríz claimed that excessive duties had raised Spanish prices to such an extent that the colonists preferred to purchase foreign goods.

In order to solve the dilemma, Uztaríz recommended that duties on Spanish goods be lowered substantially to make them cheaper than foreign commodities. In addition, he advised strengthening the navy in order to combat lucrative clandestine commercial operations. He suggested that all warships be built in such a manner that they would be capable of carrying cargo, thereby defraying some of the expense to be incurred in expanding the navy. In conjunction with these latter proposals, Uztaríz advised the crown to promote commerce, especially in textiles, by licensing royal agents in all major ports of the Mediterranean, thereby stimulating demand in these areas for Spanish products.[6]

Another important Spanish theorist of this period was Bernardo de Ulloa. He was born in Sevilla in the latter half of the seventeenth century and died in Madrid in 1740. Ulloa, like Uztaríz, was an adviser of Philip V and is considered by most colonial scholars the greatest Spanish economist of the first half of the eighteenth century. He wrote his most important treatise in 1734, _Restablecimiento de las fabricas y comercio español_.

Ulloa was greatly influenced by Uztariz. Like Uztaríz, Ulloa considered execessive taxation one of the prime causes of the decline of Spanish industry. He urged that both sales taxes and arrival-departure duties be reduced in order to stimulate the flow of trade between Spain and her thriving colonial empire. Furthermore, he proposed that drastic measures be taken to redevelop the Spanish textile industry which was the most important industry next to agriculture.[7]

Ulloa also became interested in the contraband trade. He considered the Treaty of Utrecht both a disgrace and a sham. Ulloa claimed that as a consequence of this treaty the contraband activity in the Indies had risen significantly. For this problem Ulloa saw only one solution, namely to expel the foreigners (the English and French primarily) from the Antilles, but the crown did not take his proposal seriously. As a final concern, Ulloa supported the idea of revitalized flotas and in the end advocated that the crown adopt a policy of requiring that all goods bound for the Indies ports be carried in Spanish vessels.[8]

The most dynamic minister of Philip V, at least in the area of commerce and industry, was the Spanish economist José Campillo y Cossío, Minister of War and Finance in the latter years of Philip's reign. In his treatise _Nuevo sistema de gobierno económico para la América_, he called for renewed efforts to modernize and industrialize Spain. Campillo finished his epic work in 1743, yet it remained unpublished until 1789. His book endorsed liberalization of trade as well as the radical reorganization of colonial administration. He emphasized the opportunities which Spain was missing in the Americas; her failure to exploit the economic and natural resources of her possessions, and her inability to assure Spanish subjects and products an adequate share in the colonial trade.[9] In order to bring more land under cultivation in the Indies, and thereby stimulate the agricultural sector, Campillo suggested that the Indians be given tax-free land grants. Campillo contended that lower commercial taxation would alleviate the problem of contraband. Finally, in the latter part of his book, he proposed that a regular mail service be adopted, that the Cádiz monopoly be curtailed or abolished, and that the fleet system be ended. His proposals were designed to expand commercial traffic between Spain and her colonies.[10]

In 1764, Charles III implemented one of Campillo's proposals, esatblishing a colonial maritime mail service. The Spanish port through which all colonial correspondence flowed was that of La Coruña. In the Indies, the mail initially went through Havana which became the center for the mail service. All colonial trade ships subsequently dispatched to the various mainland ports carried correspondence. In Mexico, Veracruz remained the pivotal place for mail distribution.[11]

Ferdinand VI succeeded to the throne of Spain upon the death of his father, Philip V, in 1746. He appointed Bernardo Ward as Minister of the <u>Casa de Contratación</u> in 1756 and instructed him to make a grand tour of Europe. This tour was designed to provide the king with the latest knowledge about commercial patterns extant among the various colonial powers. Ward's specific duty was to observe and record any techniques that would be useful in expanding Spanish trade and industry. Concluding his travels in 1759 and returning to Spain, Ward reported to the new monarch, Charles III.

In 1762, Ward completed a book based upon his observations which he entitled *Proyecto económico*. This book which remained in unpublished form until 1779, called for a general relaxation of Spanish commercial restrictions. Included within the text was a suggestion that the crown open more Spanish ports to the lucrative Indies trade.[12] These changes Ward reasoned would help to create an environment conducive to *comercio libre*.

Mexico had its own economic theorists. Two in particular stand out in the late colonial period--Antonio de San José Muro and José María de Quirós. Muro, a Bethanite friar who came to New Spain in 1784, became a spokesman for the middle classes in Guatemala and southern Mexico. He wrote in the *Gazeta de Guatemala* about the benefits obtained from the adoption of *comercio libre*. Muro, however, saw one detrimental affect from the initiation of *comercio libre*: the growth of monopolized merchant houses in Veracruz. With the extension of *comercio libre* in 1778, the system of flotas and trade fairs at Jalapa were ended. The mercantile community of Veracruz quickly took advantage of the situation by raising prices nearly 200 percent. Muro as a consequence advocated the establishment of regional trade fairs in Jalapa and Orizaba in order to curtail the economic power and influence of the Veracruz merchants.[13]

José María de Quirós, who served as secretary of the Veracruz consulado, wrote pamphlets concerning the advances attributable to the regime of _comercio libre_. He witnessed the economic changes which occurred after the implementation of _comercio libre_. In 1816 he completed his _Reflexiones sobre el comercio libre de las Américas_. Published in 1817 by the Veracruz consulado, the report revealed that Mexican commercial and industrial development had escalated as a direct consequence of the introduction of _comercio libre_. All major economic indicators revealed substantial development following the establishment of _comercio libre_, especially in the industrial and agricultural sectors. In addition, the previously thriving clandestine contraband trade declined radically until the Napoleonic Wars broke out.[14] In comparison to Spain, Mexico had a limited number of economic theorists in the late eighteenth century. The majority of Mexico's economic analysts were either members of the colonial bureaucracy or the mercantile professions (usually consulado connected).

Relations between Great Britain and Spain also influenced the ultimate extension of _comercio libre_. Hostilities in the eighteenth century between these two nations were aggravated by the War of the Spanish Succession (1701-1713) in which the British supported the Hapsburg claimant to the throne. The French under the auspices of Louis XIV supported the Bourbon candidate--Philip of Anjou who subsequently became Philip V of Spain. After a lengthy war in which the British captured Gibraltar and Minorca, a peace treaty was signed in 1713. Included in the Treaty of Utrecht was a concession which became infamous in Spanish history. The Spanish crown granted the asiento (the right to send one ship to the Indies each year) to the English. The asiento gave the British an open door to participate in the slave trade that was so important to the sugar plantations in the Spanish Caribbean islands. The most important consequence of this concession was Spain's inability to prevent the accompanying contraband trade.[15] The War of the Spanish Succession and the granting of the asiento did have one desireable affect. From the Spanish point-of-view it strengthened Franco-Spanish relations and led to the completion of the First Family Compact. Contained within the provisions of this agreement was a concession allowing the French to trade with Spanish overseas possessions. In addition, each nation was bound by the treaty to come to the aid of the other if attacked by the British.[16]

The most serious conflict between Spain and Great Britain in the eighteenth century was the Seven Years War (1756-1763). In February 1762, the Spanish and French Foreign Ministers signed the Third Family Compact. This treaty granted further trading concessions and military guarantees to each nation. The British government believed that Spain was preparing to enter into the war which had been raging between France and England since 1756. Subsequently in August 1762 the English captured and occupied the seaports of Havana and Manila, crucial links in Spain's international commercial empire. The Spanish and French governments, as a result of these defeats (the English forces in the Caribbean had additionally captured the principal French islands in the Antilles), sued for peace in 1763. They were forced to sign the humiliating Treaty of Paris.

Under the terms of the treaty, both Havana and the Philippines were restored to Spain, but the Spaniards were required to cede Florida to the British. Spain relinquished her claim to participate in the Newfoundland fishery. The concession causing the most serious protest in Spain was the recognition of the British right to cut logwood in the Bay of Honduras.[17] Spanish officials were fearful that the proximity of such an operation to the Mexican viceroyalty would increase smuggling activities and therefore frustrate Spanish attempts to revive trade with this area. In addition the Spanish crown was concerned that the British government would use Honduras as a military base and possibly invade Mexico. As compensation for the loss of Florida, the French crown agreed to hand over Louisiana to Spain.

In the years following the Seven Years War, the French and Spanish governments remained resolute in their desire for revenge on the British crown. Charles III was particularly adamant in his determination to end the continued illegal commercial encroachments by the English upon his empire. Between 1779 and 1783 Spain joined France in aiding the rebellious English colonists in North America in their war against Britain. After the defeat of Charles Cornwallis at Yorktown by the French admiral, Comte Francois de Grasse, the British government began to press for peace. On 3 September 1783, the English, French, and Spanish representatives signed the Treaty of Versailles. Under the conditions of the treaty, Spain recovered both Minorca and Florida from the English. The British further agreed to the dismantling of their establishments in Belize on the Yucatán peninsula.[18]

Rivalry between Spain and Great Britain in the eighteenth century increased the vulnerability of Spain's Indies trade to contraband operations. Gradually the king's ministers became convinced that no amount of tinkering with the old commercial system could free the Spanish empire from the encroachments of smugglers. With this realization, they soon adopted and became advocates of free exchange. The great strides made in Havana's trade during the British occupation of 1762, however, prompted the Bourbon crown's decision to adopt the policy of limited free trade (comercio libre). In the years prior to the British seizure, Havana averaged between five and six ship arrivals per year. The average annual yield from export and import duties collected before the capture was only 30,000 pesos. On the other hand, in the year following the capture, when the British opened the port of Havana to trade, more than three hundred ships unloaded their cargoes there, and more than 400,000 pesos in import-export duties were collected.

Noting the exceptional economic expansion during the English occupation of Havana, Charles III ordered the creation of the _Junta técnica_. The _Junta_ was composed of five technical experts in the areas of commerce and industry: the Marqués de las Llamas; Don José Moziño y Ortega, Don Francisco Craywinckel, Don Simón de Aragori, Don Pedro Goozens, and Don Tomás de Landaquiri. These experts were charged with reporting to the king on the proper course to follow in commercial reform. The _Junta_ debated whether it should recommend reforms for Spain, commerce between Spain and foreign countries, or between Spain and the Indies. The committee decided to review the problems connected with colonial commerce.

In the report presented to Charles III, the _Junta técnica_ found eight specific reasons for commercial stagnation in the Indies. A paramount obstacle to expansion of trade was the Cádiz monopoly, according to the committee. The continued existence of flotas restricted the flow of trade to the Indies because of the limited number of licensed ships (_navíos de registro_). The _Junta_ complained about the system of levying duties on liquors, the tonnage duty (_tonelada_). In addition, the committee condemned the practice of collecting _palmeo_ (duty on the volume of goods). The collection of _palmeo_ caused a distortion in some Spanish trade goods, such as textiles. The *Junta técnica* also observed a general neglect of agriculture which they attributed to the lack of sufficient slaves. The primary cause of the decline of colonial commerce, the *Junta* reported, was excessive commercial duties. The committee claimed that unjust taxation in commerce stimulated smuggling activities. In conclusion, the *Junta* decried the level of contraband trade and insisted that a solution be found.[19]

These technical experts, in addition to their criticisms, presented a group of proposals to promote commercial expansion. In their report, they advocated the liquidation of the Cádiz monopoly by opening up the privilege of the Indies trade to all the provinces of Spain. This action would facilitate development in agriculture and navigation. They proposed opening colonial trade to the following Spanish seaports: Barcelona, Tortosa, Alicante, Cartagena, Málaga, Sevilla, Vigo, Gijón, Santander, Sontonía, Bilbao, and San Sebastián. About thirty-five seaports in the Indies were proposed to be extended this privilege as well.

The committee made some additional proposals. They advocated the abolition of the flotas which were detrimental to expanded trading activities. In conjunction with the latter proposal, the *Junta* suggested that the Minister of the Indies station commercial agents in all Indies ports to spur commerce. The committee supported the abolition of most commercial duties; however, in lieu of total abolition they suggested that duties be collected on an ad valorem basis. Throughout their report the Junta advocated preferential treatment for Spanish goods. To foster agricultural activity, the committee proposed an expanded slave trade. In February 1765, the Junta técnica presented its proposals to Charles III.[20]

Eight months later, on 16 October 1765, Charles III issued the first free trade decree. The decree authorized limited free trade between certain Spanish and American ports. The Spanish ports now included in the colonial trade of the Caribbean islands were Cádiz, Sevilla, Alicante, Cartagena, Malaga, Barcelona, Santander, La Coruña, and Gijón. Initially, the islands of Cuba, Española, Puerto Rico, Margarita, and Trinidad were extended the privilege of comercio libre. Palmeo and tonelada duties were eliminated. Instead duties were collected on an ad valorem basis.[21]

On 23 March 1768, the king granted identical concessions to Louisiana. The port of New Orleans was added to the list of ports with which Spanish merchants could trade directly.[22] On 5 July 1770, the Yucatán peninsula and Campeche were brought under the umbrella of comercio libre. They gained an added privilege--they were allowed to import directly from Veracruz.[23]

In July 1772, Charles III decreed that all Spanish vessels would be free from duties if they were conveying raw cotton or textiles regardless of their point of departure.[24]

The mutual inter-colonial trade concession was granted on 20 January 1774 to Peru, New Spain, Guatemala, and New Granada.[25] Then, on 2 February 1778, Charles III extended freedom of trade (comercio libre) to Buenos Aires, Chile, and Peru.[26] On 16 March 1778, the Spanish crown expanded the free trade area to include the Canary island ports of Alfaques, Tortosa, and Almeria.[27]

The most important of Charles III's decrees, however, was the famous Reglamento y aranceles para el comercio libre issued on 12 October 1778. Comercio libre was granted to thirteen Spanish ports (the antecedent ones, plus those of Almería, Alfaques de Tortosa, Santa Cruz de Tenerife, and Tarragona). The Reglamento authorized free trade to twenty-two Indies ports: nine major ports (Havana, Cartagena, Buenos Aires, Montevideo, Valparaíso, Concepción, Arica, Callao, Guayaquil) and thirteen minor ports (Puerto Rico, Santo Domingo, Montecristo, Santiago de Cuba, Trinidad, Margarita, Campeche, Santo Tomás de Castilla, Oma, Santa María, Río de Hacha, Portobello, and Chagres). The Reglamento separated these ports into major and minor categories according to the duties they would pay. The duties for minor ports was established at 1½ percent for Spanish goods and 4 percent for foreign goods. For the major ports the duties on Spanish goods was levied at the rate of 3 percent and for non-Spanish commodities at 7 percent.[28]

Results from comercio libre were remarkable. In the

decade between 1778 and 1788, the value of trade with Spanish America increased 700 percent.[29] While the colonial merchants were critical of this new system, they later became advocates of free trade policies as their profits increased. Comercio libre caused a burgeoning of business opportunities which the colonists in Spanish America applauded. Most colonial merchants witnessed increased freedom in their business activities which they attributed to free trade. By the end of the eighteenth century Bourbon monarchs and ministers had removed most of the regulations which had retarded commercial expansion.[30]

The culmination of the Spanish free trade movement came with the extension of comercio libre to Mexico in 1789. Revillagigedo indicated in a 1793 report that after 1765 the crown had requested suggestions from colonial officials as to how best to incorporate free trade into the rest of the Spanish empire. Most Spanish American officials sent reports outlining features they liked and those which they felt should be amended to fit the local situation. In the case of Revillagigedo, he firmly believed in the virtues of the comercio libre system.

Others complained about the possible economic repercussions of adopting a free trade system. Between 1765 and 1789, the principal opponents of comercio libre in New Spain were merchants associated with the Mexico City consulado. Naturally they wished to protect their commercial privileges and opulent lifestyle. Informed of the impending implementation of comercio libre in 1786, they responded by sending a special deputation to the Madrid court to attempt to alter Charles IV's decision. Charles IV concluded, however, after careful analysis by the Conde de Floridablanca, that the advantages of a free trade system outweighed the disadvantages and extended free trade to Mexico in 1789.[31]

During the eighteenth century, the Bourbon monarchy modified the Hapsburg commercial system. Eventually the crown realized the futility of such a program. No measureable increase in Spanish transatlantic commerce had occurred. Gradually, during the Bourbon century, the Spanish crown and its ministers responded to suggestions for economic reform made by Spanish economists. Some gifted economists--Campillo, Ward, for example--were ministers. Spanish eighteenth century economic theory was altered by the introduction of enlightenment ideas. Finally, a special committee advised the king to follow Campillo's suggestions. The crown therefore introduced comercio libre into the Spanish empire. Between 1765 and 1789, the Bourbon crown authorized free trade throughout the Spanish American colonies. Relaxation of imperial commercial regulations were acclaimed by the colonial bureaucrats. The purpose of comercio libre was to improve Spain's trading position within the empire. The Spanish American colonists in general obtained greater economic freedom. An unintended outcome also resulted from the new economic freedoms. Colonial bureaucrats responded to the new commercial freedoms by implementing other policies which would augment the broad policies already established by the crown. Mexican colonial officials utilized policy to accentuate the pace of economic development.

CHAPTER II

TRANSPORTATION NETWORKS AND PUBLIC WORKS

Prior to the late eighteenth century, the consensus among Mexican officialdom was that travel along Mexico's roads was so perilous as to discourage not only the courageous but the foolhardy as well. Both the poor condition of the roads and the bands of highwaymen who traversed them hampered road travel. The *Acordada* was created in the early eighteenth century to apprehend and punish the highwaymen who terrorized Mexico's travelers.[1] To deal with the scarcity of good roads, the late eighteenth century viceregal governments undertook a massive construction and repair program. Development of roads within Mexico took precedence over all other public works projects. Crucial to commercial expansion were the roads leading to the coastal ports of Veracruz and Acapulco. The highway to Veracruz, which initially ran from Mexico City through Puebla to the seaport, became the primary public works project.[2]

Viceroy Carlos Francisco de Croix began the Bourbon program of connecting Mexico City and Veracruz with a new road network in 1766.[3] Croix ordered that all travelers on the proposed road pay a toll of 1½ reales to help defray maintenance costs. He also specified the width of the proposed highway. Each section was required to be between fourteen and fifteen yards wide.[4] While traveling through Mexico in 1774 Don Pedro Alonso O'Crouley noted that most of the new highway between Mexico City and Veracruz had been constructed. In addition, he reported that the streets within Veracruz had been repaved under the auspices of the cabildo.[5]

During the succeeding viceregency of Antonio María Bucareli, most road systems were neglected. Bucareli had more pressing matters to contend with, such as the reconstruction of the fortifications surrounding the harbor of Acapulco and other defensive concerns. Bucareli's principal activity during the 1770s was to develop an effective military force within New Spain.[6]

When Viceroy Revillagigedo arrived in Mexico in 1789, he quickly recognized the need for an improved network of highways. In a report of August 1793, he noted that the lack of good roads retarded commercial expansion. Revillagigedo emphasized development of better highway networks, since they would stimulate domestic commerce.[7] In 1791, to bring about greater fiscal management of road construction and maintenance, Revillagigedo appointed Lieutenant Colonel Pedro de Aristegui as the chief revenue official for the Veracruz highway. Aristegui immediately established toll stations along the route. Each traveler was charged a toll of eleven pesos.[8]

Among those recognized for their contributions to the

Mexican highway expansion projects of the late eighteenth century were members of the Royal Corps of Engineers. Stationed near Veracruz from the 1760s, Colonel Engineer Pedro Ponce was in the late 1780s charged with producing designs for an ancillary road to Veracruz. Ponce finished the plans for the construction of a minor road from Veracruz to Jalapa in 1792. At that time the estimated cost of such a road was 521,273 pesos.[9]

Construction of the Veracruz-Jalapa highway began in 1793, then suspended during the viceregency of the Marqués de Branciforte. Branciforte's successor, Miguel José de Azanza reintroduced the program in 1797 and in 1800 Azanza reported that the second Veracruz highway was nearly completed. Thus, during the last decade of Spanish rule, the much traveled route between Veracruz and Mexico City was favored by the existence of two separate highways.[10]

Of crucial importance to the commercial environment and the Mexican highway expansion program was the creation of independent merchants' guilds in Veracruz and Guadalajara. These consulados, which were established in 1795, were charged with three specific duties: to foster trading activities, collect economic data, and aid in the construction of roads. The Veracruz consulado membership were the principal advocates of building a second highway to Veracruz via Jalapa. In 1803, the consulado was given permission to begin work on the project which proceeded rapidly until the revolt of 1810. Estimated cost of the road was 3.5 million pesos. Funds for the second Veracruz highway were obtained partially from advertisement in the Gaceta of Mexico City. The consulado issued bonds with a 5 percent annual interest rate, financed from tolls charged all road users.[11]

Antonio Bassoco, member of the consulado of Mexico City, took full advantage of this assured return upon capital. He contributed 347,000 pesos in the road built by the Mexican consulado and another 93,000 pesos on the rival Veracruz consulado road.[12] Humboldt reported in 1801 that construction of the second Veracruz highway was nearing completion, and that this second highway was well maintained.[13]

Another major thoroughfare which influenced Mexico's domestic economy led to Toluca. Studies to determine the feasibility for the construction of a road to Toluca began in the 1760s under the aegis of Viceroy Marqués de Croix. The road was designed to facilitate the transport of corn and wheat to Mexico City. The special talents of the Royal Corps of Engineers were again conscripted. Engineer Ricardo Alymer was charged in 1768 with drafting a set of plans for the new highway. Alymer made a personal reconnaissance of the construction sites to ascertain the best methods of building the road.[14] Alymer reported his findings to the Marqués de Croix in late 1768. The viceroy instructed the engineer to revise his design. Alymer continued reworking his Toluca road plans until his transfer to Spain (Galicia) in 1785.

Bernardo Bonavía, the corregidor of Veracruz, assumed direction of the Toluca road project in 1791. Bonavía enlisted the services of military engineer Manuel Mascaró. Mascaró had reviewed the proposed project in 1777, estimating construction costs at 102,231 pesos. In January 1792, a specially convened junta surveyed the proposals made by Bonavía with reference to the Toluca highway. The junta agreed that tolls should be charged to defray the costs of construction. It stipulated that the towns of Toluca and Lerma should underwrite a portion of the expenses incurred in building the road.[15]

Viceroy Azanza wrote in the <u>Instrucción</u> to his successor that the road leading to Toluca had been completed prior to 1800. Azanza claimed that the project had been skillfully managed during his viceregency by Antonio Bassoco. Bassoco believed that the Toluca highway would aid in Mexico's commercial and industrial development. Capital funding for the construction of a road between Lerma and Ixtlahuaca was provided mainly by Bassoco.[16] Bassoco's involvement in these road projects illustrates the continuing support of the Mexican merchant elite for improvements in transportation systems.

The Mexican mercantile community realized the commercial and remunerative benefits to be achieved by supporting the transportation development program of the late eighteenth century. Participation of the Mexican consulado in road construction and maintenance financing began in 1782. A major portion of the funds for paving and maintaining Mexico's many roads were provided by the Mexican consulado members, according to Antonio Bassoco. Bassoco, a leading Mexican businessman of the late eighteenth century, reported that more than 188,982 pesos were expended between 1782 and 1795 by the Mexican consulado to maintain the roads extant in Mexico. At the close of the 1790s, mercantile involvement in Mexico's road development slackened, because most of the projects had been completed or were being finished by government entities.[17]

Viceregal government under Revillagigedo took an activist role in establishing a system of regular maintenance of all Mexico's roads. Prior to the administration of Revillagigedo, nearly all improvements on the road networks were accomplished by inhabitants of nearby towns. Beginning in November 1790, all merchants or conveyors of goods were charged a half real for each foot of pavement fronting on their businesses. Although only the municipal streets of Mexico City fell under Revillagigedo's proclamation, it became a model for the rest of Mexico. Most paving was done by convict labor from the local prisons.[18] Public bidding for construction and maintenance of Mexico's roads was almost non-existent. Revillagigedo noted in 1793, that the lack of continuity in planning road construction and maintenance resulted in deterioration of the Mexican highway system.[19]

In 1791, Revillagigedo drafted a model set of ordinances to ensure the upkeep of Mexico City's streets. Each citizen of Mexico City was expected to participate in the cleaning of the streets on Wednesdays and Saturdays. All shopkeepers were required to maintain the pavement near their place of business. The carreteros (carriage and wagon-keepers) were instructed to keep their vehicles clean so that no trash was transported from one location to another. Every carro (cart) operator paid a monthly fee of 6 pesos to revenue officers of the Mexican viceregal government for road maintenance. Households also had an obligation to maintain the street surface fronting their property.[20] In general, the system of public maintenance of roadways developed by Revillagigedo was successful.

Bridge maintenance was an important adjunct to the road maintenance program instituted by Revillagigedo in November 1790. Both the Veracruz and Acapulco highways had major bridges which were washed out continually during the eighteenth century. Construction of bridges was usually the duty of the Royal Corps of Engineers, but maintenance was normally the responsibility of the town or village nearest the structure. Finances for bridge construction and maintenance was derived principally from the Royal Exchequer.[21]

Transport conveyances for travel within colonial Mexico consisted primarily of carros (carts), coches (carriages), carretones de cuatro ruedas (wagons), and arrieros (muleteers). Arrieros were the primsry conveyors of commercial products within Mexico. In the early eighteenth century, the arrieros of the Jesuit estates around Mexico City blazed the commercial paths leading to the capital. During the initial stages of the eighteenth century, the Jesuit managed estates provided the principal demand for arrieros. With the Jesuit expulsion in 1767, demand for muleteers slackened. The hacendados who took over the former Jesuit estates became the primary users of muleteers.[22] Revillagigedo noted in 1793 that the chief importance of the muleteers arose from their ability to traverse the many roads and paths which were impassable to wagons and carts.[23]

Carretones de cuatro ruedas were used fundamentally in the caravan trade. Caravan trade conisted of a group of wagons (normally more than eight) trading with the more remote locations in New Spain. The four-wheeled wagon was used extensively for carrying goods of the Mexican mercantile houses. Wagon caravans traveled from Mexico City to Guanajuato, Durango, Valladolid, Guadalajara, Chihuahua, Perote, and Santa Fé (New Mexico). These wagon trains departed and arrived in Mexico City on an irregular basis. Wagon caravans were especially prevalent in northern New Spain where presidial soldiers accompanied them across hostile Indian territory.[24]

Carros were utilized primarily for the transport of

local agricultural produce in the late colonial Mexican economy. Carts have a long history of use within the Hispanic world. These two-wheeled vehicles were numerous in the rural locations in Mexico. Viceroy Revillagigedo observed in August 1793 the continued presence of _carros_ within Mexico even after the introduction of _carretones de cuatro ruedas_ in the late eighteenth century.[25]

Another important colonial transportation vehicle was the _coche_. In late colonial Mexico, stage coach lines linked all commercial centers. These coaches, however, carried mainly passengers and mail. _Casas de comunidad_ or _tambos_ (way stations) were constructed along the roads leading to Veracruz and Acapulco. Minor stations were established in the late eighteenth century on roads which led to Queretaro and Puebla. Because stage coaches kept regular time schedules and traveled to primarily urban centers, most colonial mail was carried by these vehicles.[26]

To promote continued expansion in commerce the viceregal government in the late eighteenth century instituted a program to bring all customhouses into conformity with the one located in Mexico City. Because of the intensified commercial operations in Veracruz in the late eighteenth century, a new customhouse had to be built to accommodate the enlarged number of revenue officials.

Once again the viceregal government enlisted the special skills of the Royal Corps of Engineers. In the spring of 1784, Viceroy Matías de Gálvez charged the Director of the Engineers, Miguel del Corral, to design a set of plans for the construction of a new customs building. Francisco Agudo, Director of the Royal Exchequer, instructed Corral to make an estimate of the funds required. Agudo further requested that Corral send him a report of the construction expenses. In the meantime, Corral had designed an alternate scheme. Instead of building an entire customhouse, Corral proposed that the Convento de los Agustinos in Veracruz be modified for customs purposes. Corral calculated that the viceregal government would save more than 20,000 pesos if it adopted his proposal. Viceroy Gálvez received the plans from Corral, however, he died in 1784 before making a decision.[27]

In August 1785, Corral was directed by the governing audiencia of Mexico City to revise his plans for the Veracruz customs building and resubmit them to a specially convened junta. Corral's specifications were approved by the junta in 1786. In 1788, Fernando Josef Mangino, the new superintendent of the Royal Exchequer in Mexico began to authorize the dispersal of funds for a new customhouse in Veracruz. Corral's previous plan to modify the Convento de los Agustinos was apparently dropped by the viceregal government sometime between 1784 and 1788. Construction of the customs building did not begin until the 1790s. Revillagigedo instructed Corral to alter his designs one more time.

Corral followed the viceroy's instructions and built a special artificial island for the customhouse. Revillagigedo was a strong advocate of public works development which aided commercial expansion in New Spain.[28]

As a part of the public works program of the late eighteenth century, the redevelopment of New Spain's defenses was important to the continued commercial expansion precipitated by the promulgation of comercio libre. Fortification construction and maintenance was primarily the job of the Royal Corps of Engineers. Such notable engineers as Ricardo Alymer, Miguel Costanzó, Manuel Mascaró, Miguel del Corral, Pedro Ponce, Juan Pagazaurtundúa, and Juan Camargo y Cavallero were involved in fortifications development at some time in their careers. The forts of Perote, Orizaba, San Juan de Ulúa, and San Diego de Acapulco were the principal defensive structures of New Spain. The forts located in Veracruz and Acapulco were crucial to the defense of Mexico's international trade, given the commercial importance of these seaports.[29] Engineer Miguel Costanzó noted in a report sent to Viceroy Azanza in January 1799 that the key to New Spain's defense was the fort of San Juan de Ulúa. Costanzó observed that many modifications had been made on the fort since 1799 to make it more secure.[30]

An important adjunct to the fortifications and public works development was the creation of the Naval Department of San Blas with its shipbuilding facilities. The department was initially established in 1767 to serve as a departure point for Spanish penetration along the northwest coast of North America. It later became an important center for trading with Alta California.

Shipbuilding projects were recognized as a vital link to military preparedness in San Blas. The first vessel constructed in San Blas was the 180 ton packetboat San Carlos completed in 1768. In 1769, a 59 ton schooner named Nuestra Señora de Guadalupe was launched from the drydock of San Blas. Other ships built by the department include the Princesa (1778), Felicidad (1785), Valdés (1790), Sutil (1791), Mexicana (1791), and Activa (1792). These sailing ships became the backbone of San Blas' Alta Cailfornia fleet.[31] Alejandro Malaspina reported in 1790 that these vessels conducted extensive business with the Alta California region.[32] San Blas' importance rested with its drydocks and naval forces. As New Spain's principal naval station in the late eighteenth century, it became crucial in maintaining the security of the Manila trade and the commerce with California.

Most of the innovations introduced in New Spain by the viceregal government in the late eighteenth century were first tested in Mexico City. Establishment of a public-lighting system was of great importance to the mercantile community in that city. Both the viceregal authorities and the Mexico City merchants believed that street-lighting would discourage crime and thereby stimulate an increase in commercial activities.

Viceroy Marqués de Cruillas was first to adopt a crude system of municipal street-lighting for Mexico City. In 1763, he issued a proclamation requiring all merchants to illuminate the patios in front of their stores. Merchants who disobeyed this order were placed in prison for a day and fined one peso for each infraction. The Marqués de Cruillas believed that public-lighting was essential to Mexico City's economic development.[33]

Don Angel María Merelo, a noted businessman of Mexico City, presented a new plan for the illumination of Mexico City's streets in May 1777. Merelo counseled Viceroy Antonio María Bucareli to choose a superintendent to oversee the street-lighting program. He also suggested that a hundred lantern keepers be hired, whose duties would consist of maintaining the lanterns from dusk to dawn. Merelo even designed a model street lamp. All shopkeepers, under Merelo's plan, were expected to keep the lanterns in front of their stores lighted.[34]

Governmental interest in the development of street-lighting in Mexico City lessened after the viceregency of Bucareli. In 1785, Viceroy Matías de Gálvez issued a series of reports on the condition of street-lighting in the capital. In Viceroy Gálvez's reports, he stressed that most of the important public buildings in Mexico City were illuminated outside. Gálvez noted one serious obstacle to the expansion of street-lighting: the government lacked sufficient numbers of lanterns. Gálvez proposed that a special factory be constructed in Mexico City to manufacture lanterns.[35] In February 1787, interim Viceroy Alonso Nuñez de Haro y Peralta observed that the Royal Lantern Factory of Mexico City was producing sufficient quantities of both street lamps and fuel. He acknowledged that all the principal streets of the capital were illuminated at night.[36] The major governmental and public buildings had street-lighting by 1790.

Revillagigedo arrived in Mexico City in 1789 and realized the need to reorganize the city's street-lighting program. He noted that the street-lighting program lacked central administration (a group of officials responsible for its daily operation). His *Reglamento* of 1790 made the Intendant-Corregidor responsible for supervising the program. He appointed the *Administrador de Guarda Mayores*, Don Josef Moreno, to oversee the guards who maintained the street-lights. Each *Guarda Mayor* was charged with inspecting and maintaining the lanterns assigned to him by the *Administrador*. The salary of a *Guarda Mayor* was 2000 pesos per annum. Any guards failing in their duties could be docked wages or required to serve guard duty at the central jail for a maximum of eight days.

Penalties for destruction or damage of the street-lights were severe. Those persons caught vandalizing the lanterns received two hundred lashes. People arrested for stealing the lanterns were given two hundred lashes and put to work repairing public buildings in the capital. Revillagigedo believed that punishment would dissuade future offenders and thereby reduce the expense of replacing lanterns.[37]

Viceroy Revillagigedo in his 1794 _Instrucción reservada_ made some observations concerning the management of street-lighting in Mexico City during his viceregency. He reported that the expenditure for the maintenance of the lanterns was 24,440 pesos yearly. Revillagigedo acknowledged that revenues to pay for the street-lamps came principally from tolls exacted from wheat transported into Mexico City. The special taxes from wheat generated 36,500 pesos in revenue. Documentation reveals that the street-light program had a surplus of 12,000 pesos during the viceregency of Revillagigedo, after all expenses were paid.[38] The foregoing statistics indicate how successful Revillagigedo was in the fiscal management of the Mexican street-lighting program. By the end of the colonial period, street-lighting had substantially curtailed crime in the capital and thereby had promoted increased commercial activity. Establishment of street-lighting within Mexico City is a good example of how the viceregal government attempted to modernize and improve municipal administration.

Public works development in Mexico during the late eighteenth century undoubtedly aided in the expansion process. The various public works projects undertaken were primarily inspired by the viceroys and other colonial officials. In planning and initiating these public works projects, the late colonial viceroys envisioned a greater pace of economic activity especially within the important urban cores. Development of road networks within Mexico made the transport of goods much easier and less time consuming. Because of these expanded highways in New Spain, the cost of shipment was decreased. In addition to these road projects, the viceregal government undertook the promotion of other projects which would lend themselves to economic and commercial expansion. Fortifications were continually modified by the Royal Corps of Engineers to make Mexico more secure from external attack. Viceroys also supported the construction of new customhouses which increased the revenue flowing into both the viceregal and royal coffers. Viceregal governments introduced a street-lighting program into Mexico City primarily to reduce the crime rate and thus foster increased commercial activities. Development of public works projects by the viceroys is among the clearest examples of how the viceregal administration promoted economic expansion in the Mexican colony.

CHAPTER III

FOOD PRODUCTION AND COMMERCIAL AGRICULTURE

Mexico has remained over the centuries a primarily agrarian based society. The eighteenth century revival of Mexican agriculture seems to have occurred because of three factors: the improvement in mining production, the increasing population, and the introduction of comercio libre. These three factors improved the profitability and productivity of agriculture and enlarged the market for agricultural produce.[1] Domestically, no other sector within the Mexican economy rivaled agriculture in terms of the wealth it generated for the Mexican populace.[2] Agricultural expansion was a preeminent concern to Mexican officialdom in the late colonial period.

The major areas of agricultural production in the central part of Mexico encompassed the localities of Tenayuca, Tlateloco, Chalco, Mexicalzingo, and Texcoco. These productive areas are noted for the high quality of their maize. In the province of Puebla, a part of the central Mexican intendancy, the jurisdictions of Cholula, Nopalucan, Coatepec, and Tepeaca produced large quantities of grains. Other areas of agricultural importance, particularly for maize and wheat production, included the regions of Toluca (Matlalzingo, Toluca), Oaxaca (Coixtlahuaca, Talistaca), Guerero (Olinala, Pajalutla), Veracruz (Coatzacoalcos, Zongolica) and those of Michoacan and Cuernavaca.[3] The prosperity of the agricultural setting was dependent upon the "circles of consumption." Commercial agriculture was centered around mining camps and the large urban centers.[4]

The concept of crop rotation greatly affected agricultural productivity by the late eighteenth century. José Antonio Alzate y Ramírez, a noted expert on Mexican development, reported in 1785 that agricultural yields on a hacienda near Yautepec had nearly doubled with the introduction of crop rotation and improved land management. Alzate claimed that crop rotation had been introduced throughout Mexico by 1785. With the continued implementation of crop rotation many harvest hacendados were able to grow a greater variety of crops. Commercial agriculturists usually produced cash crops, such as sugar and tobacco. A hacendado normally grew both a cash crop and a subsistence crop.[5] Changes in agricultural knowledge had a beneficial impact upon rural employment. With better utilization of agricultural lands, the harvest hacendados in late colonial Mexico prospered.

City-dominated consumption centers created enlarged markets for both pastoral and agricultural produce. Between 1742 and 1810 the population of New Spain nearly doubled, causing an increase in the demand for agricultural commodities. Food prices, as a consequence, continued to rise unabated during much of the eighteenth century. O'Crouley who visited Mexico in 1774, observed that Mexico City consumed each year 300,000 sheep, 15,000 head of cattle, 25,000 pigs, and an undisclosed number of chickens. In 1788, the metropolis consumed almost 1.5 million pounds of corn. In addition, the populace absorbed 1.5 million chickens, 15,300 head of cattle, 50,000 pigs, and 236,000 pounds of salted fish. Mexico City remained the most important urban market for agricultural and pastoral produce in the late Mexican colony.[6]

Other important consuming centers in late colonial Mexico included the cities of Puebla and Querétaro, each with 50,000 inhabitants. These two cities consumed approximately 600,000 fanegas of corn per year.[7] Each hacienda which produced sugar or refined silver created an instant market for foodstuffs, livestock, and fodder. As the demand for transport animals for commercial purposes rose, the need was supplied from the haciendas located in the north and the Bajío.[8]

The development of the Bajío in the late eighteenth century illustrates the dynamics of the revival of the Mexican economy. Guanajuato was the key center of silver production. Querétaro was the chief manufacturer of woolen textiles. San Miguel el Grande, Celaya, and Salamanca produced industrial textiles for export. The Bajío also included a number of productive haciendas--in 1793, a total of 448. In the corregimiento of Querétaro were located an additional 92 haciendas. Whenever possible these haciendas transferred their production activities from cereal to more lucrative livestock endeavors. Hacendados preferred raising cattle and sheep, because neither was labor intensive.[9]

In the eighteenth century the hacienda continued to be the dominant enterprise in New Spain. Hacienda labor was gained primarily through the system of debt peonage. One clear exception to the pervasiveness of debt peonage was Oaxaca, where large entailed estates existed in conjunction with Indian towns and villages. The eighteenth century haciendas tended to emphasize extensive pastoral occupations (cattle raising and sheep raising) rather than intensive crop cultivation.[10]

The profitability of the agricultural products depended to a large extent upon the location where they could be marketed. The markets in central Mexico were the most lucrative. In particular, San Miguel el Grande and Mexico City dominated the agricultural marketing system and controlled, therefore , the pricing. The large commercial houses in each city determined the prices a farmer could expect to charge. The firms of Francisco Lanzagorta, Domingo de Unzaga, and Domingo Narciso de Allende dominated the markets of San Miguel el Grande during most of the eighteenth century. These merchants in addition owned much of the land surrounding the urban center. Controlling the Mexico City markets were the commercial houses of Bassoco, Urizar, Yermo, Berrio, and Miro. These mercantile houses provided meat to the capital. Supplying meat to the city was a monopoly which the cabildo granted to the larger Mexican merchants. Because the meat supply was handled by these firms, the prices of cattle and sheep were dramatically affected.[11]

The racial or ethnic composition of the population of a specific region greatly influenced the occupational structure of the area. In the Oaxacan intendancy, during much of the eighteenth century, Indians comprised 88 percent of the population, while in the Guadalajaran intendancy the inhabitants were divided into roughly three statistically equivalent groups: Indians, Spaniards, and castas (mixed races). The central Mexican intendancy more approximated the population average where Indians composed 66 percent of the inhabitants. For the entire viceroyalty, Indians comprised 60 percent of the population. All regions in which a large Indian population existed were dominated by agriculture.[12]

Within colonial Mexico the regions which contained the best agricultural potential in the late eighteenth century were the plains between San Juan del Río and Querétaro. The most important crop of the area was maize. Yields on these lands varied considerably. On the hacienda of La Esperanza nearly 800 fanegas of corn were produced for each fanega planted. In 1802, normal yields on these lands were between 300 and 400 fanegas. In New Spain, the norm was 50 fanegas of corn per fanega planted. Only the valley of Toluca harvested more than 600,000 fanegas of corn annually. Toluca was the largest producer of maize in colonial Mexico.

Humboldt observed that maize continued to be the principal staple of the Indians in the late colonial period. The Indians of Mexico in the late eighteenth century ate two primary corn-based foods: a gruel called atole and tortillas. Corn production had expanded beyond the central part of Mexico. Humboldt noted that the northern arid lands of New Spain grew corn for local consumption.[13]

The most productive area of agricultural commodities in New Spain's northern borderlands was the province of Nueva Vizcaya. More than 349,170 fanegas of corn were harvested in 1803.[14] Agricultural production within the Interior Provinces was directed toward local consumption. But livestock raising--sheep, cattle, and mules--was also important. These commodities were traded at the annual Saltillo trade fair held in September. Even cotton was produced in the northern provinces. Its quality, however, was inferior, and it therefore had a very limited market.[15]

The productivity of Mexican soil depends heavily upon the amount of rainfall and/or the extent of irrigation. Mexico's rainy season falls between June and October. The dry season lasts eight months. Because of the long periods without rainfall, many Mexican hacendados in the late eighteenth century undertook construction of massive irrigation systems on their lands in order to ensure a sufficient supply of water for agricultural purposes. Humboldt, for example, found extensive irrigation canals around the Santiago River to irrigate the fields of the agricultural communities of Salamanca, Irapuato, and León.[16] Irrigation expanded agricultural yields significantly in the late eighteenth century.

One major Mexican foodstuff was wheat. Wheat yields were greater in the late eighteenth century than in Continental Europe. Wheat was considered a staple item by the Spaniards. It was the vital ingredient in baking the bread so important to Spanish society. Average wheat yields in late colonial Mexico were between twenty-five and thirty fanegas per acre. With the introduction of both crop rotation and irrigation the Mexican hacendados increased productivity. Both fine grain (<u>grano fino</u>) and coarse grain (<u>grano flaco</u>) were grown. Fine grain wheat was produced in Toluca, Puebla, and the Huasteca areas where rainfall was appreciable. The coarser variety of wheat, on the other hand, was grown in locations with less rainfall.[17]

Recent studies by Enrique Florescano have provided new perspectives on the dynamics of the agricultural sector of the late Mexican colony. In particular, Florescano explored the relationships between prices and poor harvests in the eighteenth century. In the drought caused famine of

1785-1786 the price of corn ranged between nine and fifteen pesos per fanega. A shortage experienced in 1796-1797 because of excessive rainfall had almost the same affect on prices. The productive lands of Chalco, Puebla, Bajío, and Toluca regions did not alleviate the recurrent food shortages in the eighteenth century, since their crops supplied local consumption needs. It was primarily the large urban centers, such as Mexico City, where food prices escalated tremendously, that experienced the shortages.[18]

The potato by the late eighteenth century was a very important staple in Mexican society. Potatoes are not indigenous to Mexico. The Spaniards introduced the potato from South America during the eighteenth century. The potato was grown in Mexico primarily for its nutritive qualities and because of its adaptability to arid climates. The cultivation of potatoes did not require extensive irrigation.[19]

Another agricultural commodity brought to Mexico by the Spaniards was sugar cane. Sugar was transplanted from the Caribbean islands soon after the Cortesian conquest of Mexico. Consumption of sugar by the Mexican population expanded markedly during the late eighteenth century. It was used extensively to produce an alcoholic beverage called aguardiente. The best areas for growing sugar were along the coasts. The most productive locations in the intendancy of Veracruz were near Orizaba and Córdoba. In the Pueblan intendancy the best area for sugar cultivation was near

Cuatlá de las Amilpas. Sugar plantations in the intendancy of Mexico were located west of Toluca and south of Cuernavaca. There, the estates of the Marqués del Valle predominated.[20]

Sugar production basically supplied a domestic market, though by the late eighteenth century Mexican sugar was traded in the international setting as well. It was not, however, as widely traded as Cuban sugar. Operating plantations remained a socially acceptable activity among the Mexican nobility in the late eighteenth century. Such notable personages as the Condes del Valle de Orizaba and Miravelle and the Marqués del Valle de Oaxaca and a few newcomers like the Marqueses of Inguanzo and Mezquital augmented their wealth with successful plantations.[21]

The cultivation of cotton was another valuable endeavor which increased in importance during the eighteenth cen-

TABLE 1 COTTON PRODUCTION IN VERACRUZ

Years	Tercios	Arrobas
1797	1256	8792
1798	539	3773
1799	420	2940
1800	700	4900
1801	250	1750
1802	372	2604
1803	293	2051

NOTE: An arroba is equivalent to twenty-five pounds. A *tercio* is valued at half a horse or mule load.

SOURCE: AHH, Consulado, leg, 917, exp. 5, Noticias estadísticas de la intendencia de Veracruz, 1803.

tury. Cotton was grown chiefly in the intendancies of Puebla, México, Valladolid, Guadalajara, and Veracruz. In 1800, the Guadalajaran intendancy produced approximately 115,270 pesos worth of cotton. The intendancy of Veracruz was probably the most important cultivator of cotton in the late Mexican colony. Between 1797 and 1803, Veracruz produced about 26,890 arrobas. As noted in table 1, the production of cotton followed a cyclical pattern. Table 1 also indicates that cotton cultivation was slackening by the end of the eighteenth century. This decline in cotton production in Veracruz in the late eighteenth century was caused primarily by the increasing demand for woolen textiles.[22]

The expansion of cotton production within Mexico received its main impetus from the eighteenth century revolution in textile manufacturing.[23] Raw cotton produced in New Spain was in demand by local textile mills. To maintain a monopoly for the Mexican textile manufacturers, the viceregal government in the 1770s issued a series of proclamations which had the affect of excluding Philippine cotton from New Spain.[24]

By the second decade of the nineteenth century, cotton production in Mexico was located primarily on the eastern coast. Approximately 243,650 arrobas of cotton were produced in the coastal area north of the Veracruz intendancy. Another 486,500 arrobas were produced in the southern region. José María de Quirós, secretary of the Veracruz consulado, reported that the value of cotton production in Mexico was 731,250 pesos in 1810. He acknowledged that most cotton went to New Spain's textile mills. Quirós also noted that cotton production was not very profitable, and that livestock endeavors were more lucrative.[25]

As an adjunct to the development of cotton cultivation, the crown and viceregal authorities attempted to foster the production of _lino_ (flax) and _cañamo_ (hemp). Bucareli initiated the promotion process with a _bando_ in 1777, proclaiming that cultivation was not to be prohibited nor suppressed as it had been in the past. Finally, in 1780, the first Director of Planting was chosen--Luis Parrilla. In 1780, the crown issued a decree establishing a Royal Factory which was to be located in San José del Chalco where flax and hemp could be grown profitably. The government sent seven technical experts from the Royal Factory of Granada to supervise the establishment of the new factory.[26]

One of the technical experts who went to New Spain subsequently drafted a model plan to enhance the cultivation of _lino_ and _cañamo_. Miguel González de Tejada recommended in 1783 to Viceroy Matías de Gálvez that special academies to promote hemp and flax production should be established. Tejada believed that these academies should be placed near urban centers. Gálvez forwarded Tejada's proposal to Domingo de Arangoiti, the fiscal of the Royal Exchequer. Arangoiti informed Tejada that the Mexican treasury did not have sufficient funds to undertake his suggestion.[27]

The experts from Granada returned to Spain in 1786. In the following year the viceregal government under Manuel Antonio Flórez suspended operations at the Royal Factory of San José del Chalco.[28] When Revillagigedo became viceroy in 1789, he modified the policy concerning the cultivation of flax and hemp. During 1791 and 1792, he instructed the intendants to allow hacendados to produce _lino_ and _cañamo_ free governmental control and supervision. Revillagigedo believed that fewer restrictions would stimulate the cultivation of flax and hemp.[29]

The succeeding viceroy, the Marqués de Branciforte, drafted a set of ordinances in 1796 to govern the cultivation of _lino_ and _cañamo_. These ordinances dramatically altered the structure of excise duties associated with flax and hemp production. Flax and hemp producers were freed from the alcabala. Most maritime duties were lifted to encourage the export of _cañamo_ and _lino_.[30] Yet when Humboldt visited New Spain in the early nineteenth century, he reported that virtually no production of _lino_ and _cañamo_ existed.[31] The attempts by the crown and viceregal authorities to foster hemp and flax production were unsuccessful.

Revival of the silk production within Mexico was another program supported by the late viceregal government. Beginning in 1790, Revillagigedo drafted proposals to encourage the redevelopment of the once prosperous silk industry.

Revillagigedo believed that such a program would lessen the economic power of the Manila merchants (these merchants maintained a monopoly of the Chinese silk trade). Concessions were granted to enterprising merchants and hacendados. The possible emergence of a strong silk industry in New Spain in the late eighteenth century alarmed the crown. The crown feared that the Mexican silk merchants would compete with the silk merchants in Spain who traded finished silk products. To allay these fears Revillagigedo suggested that the Mexican silk industry be restricted to supplying only the domestic market. In 1793, he banned the weaving of silk cloth while permitting the production of raw silk.[32] Revillagigedo was largely unsuccessful in spurring the redevelopment of silk production in New Spain.

Other important agricultural commodities produced in the late Mexican colony include pulque de maguey and tobacco. Both are notable for the revenue they generated for the colonial government. Tobacco was produced in the coastal areas of Mexico where rainfall is abundant.[33] The monopoly was established in 1765 at the recommendation of José de Gálvez. In addition an alcabala was levied on all tobacco products in Mexico, producing revenues of 3.5 million pesos in 1802. In comparison, only 7.6 million pesos were collected from the normal alcabala assessed on all goods sold.[34]

Pulque, an alcoholic product whose consumption the viceregal government tried to discourage, was produced from maguey which grew in almost all regions of New Spain. José Longiños Martínez, the naturalist of the famous Royal Botanical Expedition of 1791-1792, observed plots of maguey in nearly every Mexican village he passed by. Martínez also reported that pulque was as prevalent in the central part of Mexico as in the more remote areas. Revenues generated from the tax on pulque amounted to 760,000 pesos in 1802.[35]

From the international standpoint, cochineal was the most important commercial crop in New Spain. Grown principally in Oaxaca, Mexico's primary export was the dye derived from cochineal. Cochineal bugs were caught on the <u>nopalera</u> cactus grown on the plantations in Oaxaca. The cochineal bug was then dried and made into a powder used extensively in the eighteenth century to make a scarlet dye called royal purple. Some cochineal plantations built ovens to speed the drying process in the late eighteenth century. This dye was utilized in dyeing the world's textiles until the advent of coal tar dyes in the middle nineteenth century.[36]

Oaxacan cochineal production fluctuated during much of the late eighteenth century. The last years of the 1770s were marked by a precipitous downturn in cochineal prices. The British blockade of the Mexican Gulf ports between 1779 and 1783 trapped most cochineal dye shipments within the viceroyalty. The impaired ability to transport the cochineal dye outside Mexico caused a decline in the demand for it. As cochineal prices fell, the Oaxacan producers planted fewer *nopalera* cacti resulting in less cochineal production. The production figures for 1781 were 464,625 pounds, whereas, in the previous year, production had been 1.4 million pounds. Such a drastic drop in production can be attributed to hostilities between Spain and Great Britain from 1779 to 1783. In 1782 and 1783, the production figures began to rebound from the effects of the war. Oaxaca registered new production levels in these years, 1,035,675 and 990,000 pounds respectively.[37]

The continuing crisis in the dye trade in colonial Oaxaca during the 1780s may be in part ascribed to the following four factors. First, ecclesiastical authorities in Oaxaca attempted to place a tithe on all producers of cochineal after 1780. Second, Viceroy Martín de Mayoraga in 1780 issued a proclamation calling for an alcabala levy whenever a transaction took place. Third, the two serious famines of 1779-1780 and 1785-1787 resulted in fewer Indian cochineal producers. Many Indian cochineal producers suspended their normal operations and returned to subsistence agricultural pursuits. Fourth, the intendant system was introduced. The intendant ordinances ended the repartimiento and replaced the *alcalde mayores* with sub-delegates. The *alcalde mayores* are known to have been involved in the Oaxacan cochineal trade through surrogate merchants. This illegal involvement was one of the reasons for the crown's decision to implement the intendant ordinances in 1786.[38]

Attempts were made before 1780 to promote the dye trade. Pamphlets were written and distributed extolling the virtues of cochineal trading and production. Almost always the single cause of the decline lamented in these pamphlets was the reduction in the price paid to the producer. José Antonio Alzate y Ramírez suggested a noteworthy solution in a 1777 pamphlet: pay the Indian producer a higher price for his commodity. Alzate recommended that cochineal producers be paid two pesos above the market price.[39] Little heed, however, was paid to such recommendations.

Even with the decline in production in Oaxaca, cochineal remained the primary agricultural export of New Spain. In 1802, Mexico exported 3.5 million pesos worth of cochineal. Of the cochineal shipped abroad, 1 million pesos of it came from the Oaxacan intendancy alone. Cochineal's nearest agricultural competitor was indigo. More than 3 million pesos of indigo was exported from Mexico in 1802.[40]

Economic statistics of the late eighteenth century indicate that agricultural revenues grew significantly after the adoption of <u>comercio libre</u>. The value of corn and wheat produced at the close of the eighteenth century was approximately 20 to 24 million pesos per annum.[41] Unoccupied lands by the end of the eighteenth century were sold by the crown to prospective harvest hacendados to promote the expansion of agriculture.[42]

A valuable source showing the positive growth of Mexican agriculture in the late eighteenth century is a report made by Viceroy Revillagigedo in August 1793, He pointed to a growth in tithe collections and claimed that the policy of comercio libre was primarily responsible for the increases in agricultural production in the late Mexican colony. Revillagigedo believed that tithe collections were a reliable gauge of agricultural activity because tithing was based on agricultural production. As cited in table 2, tithe

TABLE 2 TITHE COLLECTIONS IN COLONIAL MEXICO

Location	1769-1779	1779-1789
Mexico	4,132,630 pesos	7,082,879 pesos
Puebla	2,995,601 pesos	3,508,884 pesos
Valladolid	2,710,200 pesos	3,239,408 pesos
Guadalajara	1,489,424 pesos	2,084,313 pesos
Oaxaca	719,964 pesos	843,287 pesos
TOTAL	12,047,819 pesos	16,759,771 pesos

SOURCE: AGN, Virreyes, vol. 26, Carta No. 627 (reservada), Revillagigedo II to Diego Gardoquí, 31 August 1793.

collections in Mexico increased nearly 5 million pesos between the two recorded or reported periods. This latter statistic represents a 33 percent rise in tithe collections. These statistics derived from table 2 indicate an expanding agricultural sector.[43]

Between 1779 and 1816 the value of Mexican agricultural production grew from 19 million pesos to 138 million pesos. Of this latter sum, 133 million pesos were consumed by the domestic marketplace leaving a small residue for export purposes. The figures in table 3 show the continued dominance of agriculture within the Mexican economy

TABLE 3 ESTIMATES OF MEXICO'S ECONOMIC PRODUCT, 1816

Sector	Percentages	Value/Pesos
Agriculture	61%	138,850,121
Industry	27%	61,011,818
Mining	12%	27,951,000
TOTAL	100%	227,951,000

NOTE: These estimates were made by José María de Quirós based upon annual consumption levels ca. 1791-1806.

SOURCE: AGI, México, leg. 2518, Expedientes del consulado y comercio (1817-1818), Memoria de Estatuto.

As noted in table 3, mining was the least important sector in terms of Mexico's economic product at the end of the eighteenth century.[44]

The agricultural sector of New Spain grew tremendously between 1779 and 1816. The viceroys of that period focused their efforts on the commercial aspects of agriculture. Eighteenth century colonial officials attempted to introduce new commercially feasible crops, such as flax and hemp. They also tried to reintroduce the once prosperous silk industry. These two programs were largely unsuccessful. In terms of the international commercial sector, cochineal remained the dominant agricultural commodity. Pamphlets were published in the late eighteenth century citing the gains to be made by utilizing crop rotation and irrigation. Most officials lauded such suggestions. Free trade assisted in the expansion of Mexican agriculture by eliminating commercial regulations on both domestic and international commerce and thus enlarged the market for agricultural produce. At the end of the eighteenth century, Mexico exported nearly five million pesos worth of agricultural commodities, more than any other viceroyalty. Revillagigedo claimed in 1793 that *comercio libre* was one of the chief reasons for the expansion of Mexican agriculture in the late eighteenth century. His conclusion, however, is only partially true. Other innovative policies by the late colonial viceroys also contributed to agricultural expansion in New Spain.

CHAPTER IV

INDUSTRIAL RENAISSANCE

Mexican industrialization policies were dependent in part upon those policies adopted by the crown to expand Spanish industry. Spanish industrial policies were used as a guide in formulating and implementing Mexican industrial policies. The promotion of industry in both Spain and Mexico were tied primarily to technological innovation and the increased availability of investable capital. The crown, under the auspices of Charles III, established _Sociedades económicas de amigos del país_ in Spain and Spanish America to encourage industrialization and to diseminate information about technology. At the same time, the Spanish government curtailed monopolistic control of colonial trade through the introduction of _comercio libre_. Charles III ordered the reorganization of the consulados within Spain to enlarge the market for Spanish products. The crown believed that an expanded market was needed to foster industrial production. Many of the devices utilized to promote industry in Spain were also used in Mexico.[1]

The Bourbon government was convinced joint-stock commercial companies would expand commercial and industrial opportunities and encouraged the organization of such companies. The first of these companies was the Real Compañía Guipuzcoana de Caracas, created in 1728. The crucial obstacle to industrial development, however, remained insufficient capital.[2]

In Mexico the shortage of capital was difficult to overcome because of the lack of banking institutions. The Catholic Church provided much of the capital which funded mining, agriculture, and industry in the eighteenth century. Since the church was unable to meet all the demands for investment funds, the viceregal government proposed measures to provide additional private capital for investment. For example, the first Conde de Revillagigedo suggested founding bancos de avío. He believed that such banks could supplement the amount of investable capital within Mexico. The viceroy feared that the Catholic Church exerted undue influence upon the economy because of investment and lending activities.[3]

To stimulate peninsular commercial and industrial development, the crown established the Banco Nacional de San Carlos (National Bank of Spain) in June 1782. The major portion of the funds to initiate this Spanish bank came from the Mexican community. The towns of San Juan and Santiago each gave or invested twenty thousand pesos. Tejeji de la Seda remitted eight thousand pesos to Spain for investment. Sixty-three villages in Oaxaca invested nineteen thousand pesos in the San Carlos National Bank. All the Oaxacan villages providing funds for the Bank of San Carlos had one thing in common: they were Indian towns. From the customhouse account in Veracruz the village of Zimatlán committed sixteen thousand pesos. The last remaining source of Mexican funds came from the urban center of Valladolid. That city contributed fifteen thousand pesos for investment in the San Carlos Bank. The San Carlos Bank provided hardly any direct investment monies for Mexican expansion. The Bank of San Carlos invested large amounts in Spanish industries. In Mexico the Banco Nacional de San Carlos limited its operations to overseeing the bullion shipments (the bank was granted a monopoly in the transport of specie from Spanish America to Spain).[4] The chief bankers of Mexico remained the Catholic Church, the major mercantile houses, and the large hacendados.

The principal architects of Mexico's eighteenth century industrial expansion were the colonial officials and merchants. The viceroys were the most visible proponets of industrialization. Two eighteenth century viceroys stand out in the promotion of industry: Antonio María Bucareli and the second Conde de Revillagigedo. The main tools utilized by the viceregal government in directing industrial policy consisted of government contracts, patents for machinery, and commercial regulations.

In the administration of Viceroy Bucareli, two decisions are notable with regard to expanding Mexican industries. Bucareli liberalized the trade restrictions on cotton textiles. Cotton textiles were freed from all commercial duties. This action spurred cotton textile production after 1771.[5] Bucareli met regularly with Mexico's obraje (workhouse or factory) operators to discuss future industrialization and possible changes in governmental policies. In the spring of 1775, he advised the merchants of San Luis Potosí not to construct an obraje. He indicated that San Luis Potosí's textile market was not large enough to merit such a project.[6] The merchants apparently followed his advice since no obraje was built. The expansion of obrajes in the late Mexican colony was directed principally where the demand for textiles was largest--in the large urban centers.

Other examples of viceregal involvement in the promotion of industry can be found in the administration of Revillagigedo. In 1790, this viceroy granted Don Manuel Ochoa, a merchant of the Mexico City consulado, a license to manufacture and use a new machine to spin silk. Ochoa had requested a license initially from Viceroy Manuel Antonio Flórez, who had failed to respond to the request. The merchant wanted a ten year concession which he succeeded in gaining from Revillagigedo. Ochoa gave the patent for the machine to the gremio de hiladores (artisan guild of spinners). Both Ochoa and Viceroy Revillagigedo believed that new machinery would enhance silk production.[7] Another important innovation introduced by Revillagigedo to promote industrial development was the founding of a spinning school in Tixtla, a town near the capital. Its main responsibility was to teach the processes needed to manufacture cotton, silk, and woolen cloth.[8]

The viceroys of the late eighteenth century are noted for the candor with which they describe the nudity of the indigenous population, the principal laborers of the viceroyalty. One viceroy distinguished himself in his attempts to discourage nudity within Mexico. Viceroy Revillagigedo, alarmed and shocked at the level of nudity within New Spain upon his arrival in 1789, was especially disgusted at the extent of nudity within Mexico City. To suppress this practice, Revillagigedo proclaimed that the administrative heads of the _Real Aduana_ and _Casa de Moneda_ were responsible for ensuring that their employees were properly clothed.[9] This order and other similar decrees changed Mexican urban clothing habits overnight. It also enlarged the demand for manufactured cloth.

Governmental promotion of industry was not only limited to the actions of the viceroys. The intendants, created in 1786 by royal decree, were charged in their charter with the responsibility for guaranteeing continued commercial, agricultural, and industrial development within their designated jurisdictions.[10] An important adjunct to the intendant's job was to keep the crown and the viceroy informed about the progress of Mexican industry. Contained within the Intendant Ordinances of 1786 was a very important stipulation. Each intendant was instructed to compose a special report stating in detail the extent of industrial activities within his jurisdiction. The report was to be compiled either by the intendant's subordinates or the Royal Corps of Engineers.[11] Intendants were also cautioned to guard against a few individuals monopolizing an area's industries. An intendant could recommend that such individuals be refused licenses.[12]

The entrepreneurial classes also took part in the process of developing industries. In 1776, a special junta convened in Guadalajara. Composed of major merchants and landowners of the city, the junta was to decide what industries would be the most advantageous for this region. The junta recommended encouraging the wool, cotton, and fur industries. They estimated the required capital to initiate this program to be forty thousand pesos.

The members of the junta were Don Francisco J. Vizcarra, the Marqués de Pánuco, Don Manuel Ibargoyen, Don José Alfonso Lenero, Don Ramón Fernández Berrena, Don José Trigo, Don Joaquin Ibarreta, and Don Juan Angel Ortíz. To promote these industries they established a special commercial company, with each member of the junta contributing five thousand pesos. The project ended in failure. Two years later the company was formally dissolved, even though one hundred additional tailors had been brought to Guadalajara during the life of the corporation.[13]

The great mercantile houses tended to dominate all

the profitable areas of the economy, such as mining, industry, and trade. The merchant community by the late eighteenth century encouraged economic diversification. Industry was an important part of the diversification process.

Domestic industries within New Spain were much more important to commercial development than the mining sector. In 1816, the industrial sector was valued at sixty million pesos, whereas mining was valued at only twenty-seven million pesos.[14] Mining's influence upon economic growth in late colonial Mexico has been overemphasized. It is true that the Spanish government relied upon regular bullion shipments to forestall Spain's bankruptcy. The principal value of the Mexican mining industry was the currency it helped place in circulation. In addition, mining production increased employment levels within Mexico.

Information concerning industrial development comes from several sources. Intendants and viceroys were required to submit detailed reports to keep the crown and the associated bureaucracy abreast of colonial conditions. The intendants normally compiled these reports either at the request of the viceroys or the crown. The consulados also kept itemized records since they were the chief beneficiaries of the prosperity existing in the late eighteenth and early nineteenth centuries. Humboldt's writings fit into a specific category since he was the special representative of Charles IV. This traveler was allowed access to many of the documents of the late eighteenth century, including the documents housed in the Mexico City archive.

During the administration of Viceroy Revillagigedo in the early 1790s, a number of attempts were made to amass data concerning the industrial activities extant in Mexico. In 1793, Revillagigedo instructed the intendants to compile a special report concerning their regions. The viceroy sought to use this information in making his reports to the secretary of the Council of the Indies.

Manuel de Flon, the intendant of Puebla, wrote an analytical report for Revillagigedo in 1794 listing all the major industries in Puebla. Flon had been appointed in 1785 and in the interim period had become a very experienced administrator.[15] Puebla was one of the key industrial centers in the late Mexican colony. Two cloth factories with 1,177 looms and 3 glass factories were located in the Puebla area. In addition, the province had 14 yellow porcelain factories, 16 fine porcelain (<u>loza fino</u>) factories, 9 woolen blanket factories, 13 hat factories, 40 meatpacking houses; Flon also noted that the urban center of Puebla had 14 flour mills.[16] The city of Puebla was the industrial and commercial center of the intendancy. Flon reported that the other towns within the Pueblan intendancy had only limited industries. The city of Tehuacan, for example, had only 3 flour mills and 2 sugar mills. The remainder of the province had a non-industrial base.[17]

In the intendancy of Oaxaca, intendant Don Antonio de Mora y Peysal observed that Oaxaca's industries were similar to those in the province of Puebla. Most industry in Oaxaca was linked to agriculture or textiles.[18] As table 4 indicates, Mora reported thirty-one flour mills operating in the province in 1794. These flour mills produced for the great

TABLE 4 FLOUR MILLS IN OAXACA, 1794

Location	Number of Mills
Nexapa	7
Teposcolula	10
Miahuatlan	2
Huizo	3
Tecocuilco	2
Four towns, of the Marquesado de Oaxaca	7
TOTAL	31

SOURCE: AGN, Historia, vol. 74, exp. 10.

urban centers of Oaxaca. Only one sugar plantation (San Nicolas Ayotla) existed in the entire intendancy. Oaxaca, however, did have forty sugar mills which serviced this plantation.

In Oaxaca, most of the industry was centered around Tehuantepec and the city of Oaxaca in 1794. Tehuantepec had two indigo factories. One belonged to the heirs of the late Sebastián de Lorran (a noted cochineal and indigo merchant of Oaxaca) and the other to Colonel José Miguel Bejarano, the head of the Oaxacan militia. In the capital of Oaxaca, were five hundred looms which produced primarily women's cotton shawls. These factories were important for the fine quality of their product. Some officials believed these families produced textiles superior to those of Mexico City or Puebla.[19]

In the intendancy of Valladolid, thirty-four obrajes produced wool and cotton blankets. Intendant Phelipe Días de Hortega reported in 1794 that textile manufacturing was the principal occupation in the province of Valladolid. The city of Valladolid was the focal point of the industries in the intendancy. Located in the province of Valladolid were sixty-five flour mills, eighty-six sugar plantations, and eighteen indigo plantations.

Within the intendancy of San Luis Potosí, no large scale enterprises which manufactured textiles were extant in 1794. Intendant Bruno Díaz de Salcedo observed that only one obraje (hacienda de Zacala) existed within the province. The remainder of the cloth manufactured within the intendancy of San Luis Potosí was produced on the haciendas of Bocas, Peñasco, and Pozo. The textile production on these haciendas was retained for local consumption. Also within the jurisdiction of San Luis Potosí were eight flour mills (Bledos Altos, Bledos Bajos, Pila, Zavala, Ventilla, Villela, Gogorron, and San Juan de Villegas).[20]

The rich mining intendancy of Zacatecas had little industry in 1794, according to intendant Josef de Peón Valdés. Valdés claimed that only the municipalities of Zacatecas, Fresnillo, and Sombrerete showed any visible signs of industrialization. Located in the _partidos_ of Zacatecas were a total of eleven flour mills. These mills constituted nearly all the industry of Zacatecas and produced principally for the local market.

The other important mining intendancy of New Spain was Guanajuato. Guanajuato in comparison to Zacatecas was a prime example of the industrialization process in the late Mexican colony. The main industrial centers of Guanajuato in 1793 were San Miguel el Grande (nine factories), Acámbara (fifteen factories), and Villa de León (three factories). The primary manufacture of Guanajuato was blankets. Smoked hams were also produced in the intendancy, yet these were not equal in quality to those produced in Puebla.[21]

By far the most important single textile manufacturing center in late colonial Mexico was Querétaro. The fabrication of woolen textiles contributed immensely to the development and prosperity of this province and city. Querétaro was recognized for the quality of its merino wool (a special kind of wool pioneered in the Iberian peninsula). In addition to the textile factories located in Querétaro, was a cochineal dye processing plant run by Don José de Gandará. The dye industry was an important adjunct to the textile industry. Querétaro's textiles were noted for their brilliant colors.[22]

The nineteen textile factories in Querétaro employed nearly six thousand people. The average size of each plant varied between 6 and 20 looms. The larger enterprises owned the majority of the looms. The total number of looms was 280. These looms annually produced approximately seven thousand pieces of cloth which were valued at more than 500,000 pesos in 1815. In addition to these larger enterprises, smaller textile producing units called <u>trapiches</u> also existed. These smaller organizations employed an additional 3 to 4 thousand people. In these small textile mills 1,000 looms produced woolen blankets and mantles.[23] Some historians have drawn comparisons between this system and the English "cottage" industry system. This conclusion, however, is erroneous for these factories were not home based but rather were located in established structures.

At the end of the eighteenth century, the 20 <u>obrajes</u> and 300 <u>trapiches</u> in Querétaro consumed 46,000 arrobas of wool. This wool in turn produced 6,000 pieces or 226,000 yards of finished cloth. In addition, 280 pieces of coarse cloth were produced; approximately 18,000 yards. This finished cloth was valued at close to 600,000 pesos. The Querétaro textile mills also consumed a great amount of raw cotton. In 1802, approximately 200,000 arrobas were utilized to produce women's shawls and mantles.[24]

The most important report concerning the condition of Querétaro's textile mills sent to the viceroy came from the intendant. One such report stands out. In 1802, Miguel Domínguez, the Intendant-Corregidor of Querétaro, wrote to

Viceroy Félix Berenquer de Marquina citing the problems connected with the obrajes. Domínguez echoed the complaints of his predecessors. He claimed that he was overworked. Dominguez was especially critical of the Querétaro obraje operators which attempted to resist his inspections.[25]

In Querétaro, the factories followed a policy which all the intendants denounced. These factories granted advances on wages. The intendants noted that this practice marked the beginning of debt peonage (peonaje) within the city of Querétaro and its environs. Once the worker was in debt and unable to liquidate his debts, the proprietor of the obraje began to bind him in figurative or penal servitude. Intendant Domínguez acknowledged that the proprietors of the textile obrajes adopted a system of piecework so as to keep the worker indebted. In addition, the children of an indebted laborer were sometimes placed in service in the obrajes to liquidate the parent's indebtedness. The intendant did not condemn the obrajes for entirely humanitarian reasons. The intendant was responsible for the collection of tribute and other associated taxes. His job was severely complicated with the advent of debt peonage. He was almost completely unable to collect tribute payments.[26] The problem was magnified within urban centers.

Intendant Domínguez stated in his 1801 report that the Royal Tobacco Factory of Querétaro had experienced success in its program to end wage advances and debt peonage.

The factory ceased granting advances of wages to employees in the 1790s. Merchants anticipated a loss of business. The administrators of the tobacco factory feared a labor shortage would result in wages were not advanced. In 1801, Domínguez reported that the reverse had occurred. No scarcity of workers for the tobacco factory existed. Business activity near the factory increased, according to local artisans. Domínguez, therefore, recommended outlawing the practice of giving advances on wages and debt peonage.[27]

By 1816 textile manufacturing was the single most important area of the Mexican industrial sector. Wool and cotton textile production was valued at 10.4 million pesos. Woolen textiles alone accounted for 7.4 million pesos of the textiles produced. A conservative estimate of cotton textile production in 1800 was 3 million pesos. The nearest industry in both importance and revenue generation was the manufacture of bread which earned 9 million pesos in revenue.[28] Clearly, textiles dominated the industrial field.

Most Mexican industries grew significantly during the late eighteenth century. The smoking of hams and other meats was an important industry in the late Mexican colony. In Puebla, more than 200,000 arrobas of solid hams were produced each year. The Guadalajaran intendancy in 1802 netted over 260,000 pesos from ham production.[29] In 1816 the total value of ham production was 3,394,772 pesos. The tallow and hides from cattle and sheep yielded approximately 11 million pesos in receipts. The transport industry was another prosperous activity, earning over 6 million pesos in 1816. Shoe production was valued at nearly 4 million pesos at the conclusion of the eighteenth century. One last industry completely unconnected with the royal monopolies was the production of firewood and carbon which grossed 6.5 million pesos annually for its producers.[30]

Mexico even had an emerging lumber industry in the late eighteenth century. This industry was located principally in the intendancy of Veracruz because of the abundance of a great variety of trees. A lumberyard was located near the wharves at Veracruz. Most of the good was transported to Spain for ship construction. The mercantile house of Bassoco dominated this industry in the 1790s.[31] Lumber production was valued at 850,000 pesos in 1816. The manufacture of iron and steel was relatively a new technology in the late eighteenth century. In 1800, the amount of steel and iron produced was valued at approximately 883,425 pesos annually.[32]

The Royal Tobacco Factories were the preserve of the crown. Tobacco was a royal monopoly from which the crown gained much revenue. At the end of the eighteenth century, tobacco factories were located in Durango, Guadalajara, Mérida, Orizaba, Puebla, Valladolid, Veracruz, Oaxaca, and Real del Rosario.[33] In 1802 the total value from the sale of cigars was 4,686,834 pesos. The expenses incurred during fabrication amounted to 1,285,000 pesos plus the salaries

TABLE 5

DOMESTIC INDUSTRIES IN MEXICO, 1816

Products	Value/Pesos
Woolen Textiles	7,401,000
Cotton Textiles	3,000,000
Hats	500,000
Lace	150,000
Dyes	100,000
Silversmith's Products	300,000
Sheet Metal	50,000
Chinguirito and Mescal	1,800,000
Ham	3,394,772
Calf Hides	4,500,000
Spanish Leather	6,562,500
Belts	50,000
Carriages	650,000
Rigging	100,000
Mats and Baskets	250,000
Bread	9,000,000
Fish Products	150,000
Chocolate	830,078
Wax	39,843
Hunting Goods	100,000
Lime	850,000
Bricks	500,000
Chinaware	500,000
Firewood and Charcoal	6,500,000
Timber	850,000
Iron and Steel	883,425
Musical Instruments	150,000
Games	200,000
Wax Figures	50,000
Shoes	4,000,200
Salt	500,000
Ice	400,000
Gunpowder	700,000
Transport (arrieros)	6,000,000
TOTAL	61,011,818

SOURCE: AGI, México, leg. 2518, Expedientes del consulado y comercio (1817-1818), Memoria de Estatuto.

of the employees of the factories which totaled 749,000 pesos. In addition to these costs was the purchase price of the raw tobacco, which amounted to 594,000 pesos. The net profit to the king from his Mexican tobacco factories was approximately 4 million pesos in 1802.[34]

Probably one of the most important decisions regarding cigar production was made by Viceroy Bucareli in 1777. Bucareli, with the consent of Charles III, decided to suppress cigarette production and establish one hundred tobacco stands to promote the sale and consumption of cigars (puros). These tobacco stands were placed near the viceregal palace during the 1770s and 1780s.[35] They were finally moved to the Plaza del Volador during the vicregency of Revillagigedo.

While in Mexico Humboldt made an inspection of the Queretaro tobacco factory in 1803. Humboldt visited the factory to gain first-hand knowledge about the manufacture of various tobacco products so that he could more accurately report to Charles IV. The Querétaro factory employed three thousand men and nineteen hundred women. Humboldt found the buildings much cleaner than the textile mills he had seen in Querétaro. The tobacco factory had one serious defect. It was poorly ventilated. Humboldt reported that total tobacco revenues from the Querétaro factory in 1803 were two million pesos.[36] The expansion of the tobacco industry was one of the most promising programs of the viceregal government in the late Mexican colony.

Another industry over which the crown maintained a commercial monopoly was that of the production of black powder or gunpowder. A factory was constructed near Santa Fé in 1780, utilizing the plans drafted by military engineer Miguel Costanzó. This site, near the aqueduct of Santa Fé, was chosen for a specific reason: the hydraulic machinery used in gunpowder manufacturing required water to run it. Eighty mestizo boys were employed at a wage of two and a half reales per day to operate the mill according to Humboldt. The sulphur necessary for black powder production came from the volcanos near Orizaba and Puebla.[37]

The profits from the gunpowder monopoly were surprisingly volatile except in times of war. In 1792, the revenue from black powder sales was 145,000 pesos. By 1798 the profits from gunpowder sales had grown to 207,104 pesos. In comparison to the tobacco monopoly, the gunpowder monopoly remained inferior since the crown collected 14 million pesos from the tobacco monopoly. The gunpowder monopoly grew rapidly after 1800 with the onset of war. For 1801 and 1802 the gunpowder factory yielded 785,000 and 750,400 pesos respectively.[38] At the conclusion of the eighteenth century, the gunpowder industry averaged 700,000 pesos in revenues annually.[39] During the times of peace the demand for gunpowder slackened.

Viceroy Revillagigedo had noted in his Instrucción reservada that average yearly revenues from the powder monopoly in the 1790s were about 500,000 pesos. Because the expenses of the gunpowder factory amounted to 300,000 pesos, the net profit was 200,000 pesos. The expenses of the factory were distributed in the following manner: 70,000 pesos for the salaries of the employees, 40,000 pesos in gastos (expenses or fees of operation), 150,000 pesos to purchase ingredients, and 40,000 pesos for the costs of fabrication.[40] Black powder production was one of the chief industries which generated revenue for the crown. The crown therefore promoted its use and production.

It was principally the increasing monetization of the Mexican economy which caused the revival of the silver industry in the late eighteenth century. The Mexican silver production was divided into three distinct stages: the extraction of the mineral, refining ang amalgamation, and the minting of silver coins. Viceroy Revillagigedo in 1793 attributed the spurred demand for silver coinage to the heightened commercial activities resulting from the implementation of comercio libre. Increased demand for silver for commercial purposes in turn led to a further expansion of the mining industry. By the late eighteenth century, mining activities had expanded beyond the area around Guanajuato and Zacatecas into the distant lands of Sonora and Culiacán.[41]

The Royal Mint at Mexico City may be considered another crown sponsored industry. Beginning in 1733, Royal Exchequer officials began to operate the mint once again.

Prior to this date the crown had farmed out the operations. The mint employed between 350 and 400 workmen. Humboldt visited the mint during 1803. He reported that the workmen were able to produce all the money Mexico needed with only a minimum of activity. Machinery within the mint in 1803 consisted of ten rollers moved by mules, forty-two cutters, nine adjusting tables, twenty machines for marking the edges of the coins, twenty stamping presses, and five mules for amalgamating the washings and filings called _mermas_.[42]

In 1794, almost 22 million pesos were coined. This production statistic represents the average for the late eighteenth century. Average monthly production was approximately 2 million pesos. In November 1794, the mint was able to coin the enormous sum of 2,969,658 pesos.[43] Very little silver or gold was exported. On the contrary, most silver was coined for domestic purposes. The introduction of _comercio libre_ led to the expansion of mint production in the late eighteenth century. In the period between 1765 and 1778 the mint coined more than 203 million pesos. Following the adoption of _comercio libre_, production between 1779 and 1791 rose to more than 252 million pesos.[44] The mint's output, therefore, rose significantly with the advent of _comercio libre_.

In general, the era following the establishment of _comercio libre_ was the most prosperous for the Mexican economy. Industry was a principal beneficiary of this system, because it tended to reduce the level of contraband and increased domestic industrial production. The second Conde de Revillagigedo reported in 1793 that comercio libre had enhanced Mexican industrial expansion. He acknowledged that comercio libre had helped in the expansion of the textile industry both in Spain and Mexico.[45] By the second decade of the nineteenth century, Mexican industrial production was valued at sixty-one million pesos. The majority of Mexico's industrial goods were consumed internally. The industrial sector of the Mexican colonial economy was oriented towards domestic needs.[46]

The primary proponents of industrialization within the Mexican setting in the late eighteenth century were the viceroys and other colonial officials. The viceregal government utilized government contracts, patents for machinery, and reduction of commercial regulations to spur industrial activity. New machinery helped to expand Mexican productivity and was a major concern to the late colonial viceroys. The viceroys also met with Mexico's industrialists to discuss future industrialization and possible shifts in government policy. Most industrial capital came from the Mexican merchant elite and the Catholic Church. The Mexican mercantile community followed a diversified investment program to protect themselves from possible reversals in agriculture or commerce. The reports of the intendants indicate that most Mexican industries were located near the commercialized urban markets. Textile production was the chief industry in the late Mexican colony. Other important industries included tallow, lumber, firewood, leather, and porcelain. Crown sponsored industries such as cigar and gunpowder production and minting significantly expanded their operations in the late eighteenth century. Mexico's industrial sector grew markedly under the influence of enlightened viceregal policies. By the end of the Bourbon century, the Mexican industrial sector was second only to agriculture within the Mexican economy.

CHAPTER V

COMMERCIAL REVIVAL

The cornerstone of Spanish commercial theory and policy during much of the colonial era was the idea of control. Control was initially used as a device to enhance Spanish peninsular economic activity. It later became a policy utilized to liquidate the economic encroachment of the other developing nations, such as Great Britain and France. Charles III recognized the futility of this policy and initiated the program of economic liberalization in commerce with the free trade decrees of 1765, 1774, and 1778. Mexico was extended these privileges in 1789. The viceroys of the late eighteenth century embraced comercio libre enthusiastically and energetically developed policies to augment it.[1]

Mexican merchants were unable to assert themselves until the beginning of the eighteenth century. New Spain's international trade was dominated by the Cádiz and Sevillian merchants prior to the eighteenth century. With the introduction of a trade fair in Jalapa in 1720, the situation changed. No longer did Cádiz and Sevilla dominate the external and internal trade of Mexico. In April 1728 the crown stipulated that the next trade fair would take place in Jalapa, even though there had been some contemplation of transferring the fair to Orizaba.[2]

Whether a trade fair took place in Jalapa depended upon the arrival of the flotas. Between 1720 and 1778, when the fleet system was abolished, thirteen flotas appeared in the port of Veracrúz. These flotas failed to arrive on a regular basis. They entered the harbor of Veracruz at intervals of two, three, four, or even five years. Goods destined for the Jalapa fair were free from all duties (alcabala, _avería_, _unión de armas_, and _Armada de Barlovento_). Those goods not passing through Jalapa paid an 8 percent alcabala duty. In general, peninsular merchants marked up the prices of their goods between 300 and 500 percent. Mexican merchants responded by raising the prices on their export commodities.[3]

Between 1765 and 1778, three trade fairs occurred in Jalapa. Merchants in the 1760s circumvented the fleet system by engaging in the contraband trade. From 1776 to 1778 twenty merchant ships were sent to Havana carrying more cargo than this single island could possibly consume. Some of these ships, before arriving in Havana, made illicit trips to Mexico. This practice seems to confirm the prevalence of an illegal trade with Mexico in the absence of the _comercio libre_ which Cuba enjoyed.[4] Penalties for involvement in clandestine trading activities were severe. Punishment could range from simple banishment or imprisonment to loss of limb.[5] Even with these severe penalties, the contraband trade continued almost unabated. Since Mexico was excluded from the full benefits of _comercio libre_, it was a prime target for smuggling activities.

In the 1770s Viceroy Bucareli attempted to rectify some of the problems existing in the fair of Jalapa. Bucareli lengthened the time limitation to unload and transport the goods from Veracruz to Jalapa. A proclamation of 1772 stipulated that goods destined for Jalapa had to be delivered within a two month period. Furthermore, the period during which the goods remained duty free was lengthened. Bucareli considered these actions the best means available to solve existing problems and extend commerce.[6] The last convoy arrived in Veracruz in January 1778, and subsequently a fair was held in Jalapa. The value of the goods traded at this final fair was 26,924,499 pesos.[7]

With the demise of the convoy system the trade fairs in Jalapa declined. Between 1784 and 1787, the crown adopted a program of limiting tonnage within the seaports of the Mexican Gulf. Free trade decrees had the effect of allowing merchants to purchase their goods directly from Veracruz, Puebla, Mexico City, or even Jalapa. In 1786 the king finally eliminated the necessity of using Jalapa as an entrepôt.[8] Jalapa responded to the royal decree of 1786 by commemorating the event with a special fiesta and dancing in the streets.[9] On 28 February 1789 the king extended _comercio_ libre to Mexico. At this time the crown also stipulated that all Spanish manufactured goods entering New Spain would be assessed a lower duty than those goods of non-Spanish origin, which would be charged 10 percent more.[10]

The other major outlet for Mexico's international trade was the trade fair held each year at Acapulco. Usually this fair occurred between 20 January and 25 February. This city was the entrepôt for the fabled Manila Galleon trade. The Acapulco fair began in 1565 and remained a viable institution until 1817. It was probably the trade fair most closely associated with the international economy. Many of the commodities entering New Spain through the Philippines trade were available from other sources.[11]

In 1784 a group of Manila based merchants successfully petitioned the crown for permission to establish a consulado.[12] This consulado was created principally to facilitate increased commercial interaction between the Philippine Islands and Mexico. In the following year the crown authorized the establishment of the Real Compañía de Filipinas. Much of the capital to establish this special company came from the Mexican mercantile community and the merchants of Cádiz. The merchants of Cádiz were the most visible competitors of the Mexican merchants in the Philippines trade.

Even with all the commercial concessions, most trade remained controlled in one manner or another. In 1791 Revillagigedo reported that he had granted the Philippine trade an upper limit of 500,000 pesos free of duties. He also noted that the Manila trade was no longer restricted to one ship. Prior to this date the viceregal government had authorized only one annual ship to trade with the Philippines.[14] The Manila Galleon remained until the conclusion of the eighteenth century both a lucrative and important segment of Mexico's international trade. At the end of the eighteenth century, the Manila trade was valued at more than 1.5 million pesos per year.[15]

Internal trade was also dominated by the institution of the trade fair. Most notably, the trade fairs held at San Juan de los Lagos and Saltillo, dominated internal commerce. The merchants of Querétaro, San Luis Potosí, San Juan del Río, Valle de Santiago, Celaya, Guadalajara, Valladolid, Aguascalientes, and Zacatecas took their wares to Saltillo to sell them. Some of these merchants enjoyed profits in excess of 200 percent.[16] The large mercantile houses located in Veracruz, Puebla, and Mexico City tended to control the consignment trade of the more remote locations of New Spain, such as Zacatecas.[17]

The collection of alcabala in the late eighteenth century is probably the most reliable gauge of the expansion of domestic commerce. In August 1793, Revillagigedo wrote a report examining the development of the Mexican economy. As illustrated in table 6, alcabala collections rose significantly after 1778. Revillagigedo attributed the increase in

TABLE 6 ALCABALA COLLECTIONS IN NEW SPAIN

Years	Pesos
1765-1778	19,844,053
1779-1791	34,218,462

SOURCE: AGN, Virreyes, vol. 26, Carta No. 627 (reservada), Revillagigedo II to Diego Gardoquí, 31 August 1793.

alcabala to the advent of comercio libre. Revillagigedo's statistics show that in the thirteen years following 1778 alcabala collections grew by 72.4 percent. Growth in alcabala collections indicates that Mexico's domestic commerce expanded markedly in the late eighteenth century.[18]

Commerce and mining were the principal vehicles for upward social mobility in the late Mexican colony. Precise statistics of those engaged in mercantile activities are not always readily available. The census of 1791 revealed that 1,384 commerciantes resided in Mexico City.[19] With the introduction of comercio libre, the sphere of influence of the Mexico City mercantile establishments lessened to a certain degree. Notably, the Veracruz mercantile houses, which grew in number as a result of comercio libre, bypassed the Mexico City merchants and dispatched their wares into the interior of the country. No longer did the Mexico City merchants control both the international and domestic sector of the Mexican economy. Veracruz became the center for international trade following the implementation of comercio libre in 1789.

The commercial houses of Bassoco, Urizar, Yermo, Berrio, and Miro were the dominant concerns in Mexico City prior to the implementation of comercio libre. These houses remained the most important mercantile firms in Mexico City throughout the remainder of the colonial era. Little evidence exists to support the contention that these larger merchants were seriously challenged in the capital by the smaller merchants following extension of comercio libre. Although the Mexico City merchants were able to remain dominance of the capital's markets they lost control of nearly every market in the provinces. The provincial traders preferred to trade with the Veracruz merchants.[20]

Antonio Bassoco, the patriarch of the Mexico City mercantile concern of the same name, is a good example of the affects of comercio libre upon the merchant elite. Bassoco was a Basque merchant who amassed a great fortune through such diverse business activities as the China trade, the mines of Bolanos and Zacatecas, public works funding, raising livestock, and harvest haciendas. In the 1780s Bassoco undertook a disastrous export-import deal which cost him nearly a half million pesos. He became determined to abandon his international commerce for more secure investments, such as agriculture and silver mining.[21] Even with the losses suffered in the 1780s, the mercantile firm of Bassoco remained a participant in the Veracruz wood trade. Bassoco was involved in procuring timber for shipment to Spain and Havana for shipyard construction. The intendant of Veracruz knew that Bassoco was the best merchant to obtain the necessary cedars of Bejarano.[22] The lumber was sold in the <u>almacén</u> (marketplace) of Veracruz, a special marketplace constructed in the 1760s.

Many rich merchants, miners, and landowners backed off from the risky international trade following the adoption of <u>comercio libre</u>. Much of the Mexican nobility, including many merchants, such as the Condes de Agauyo, Regla, Fagoagas, Jala, Rabago, Rivas, Cacho, and Tepa, began to emulate their European counterparts. They acted more like rentiers (those who received their incomes from portfolio investment) than the more active merchants, miners, and agriculturalists of the early eighteenth century.[23]

Even with the change toward mercantile activities, peninsulares continued to control at least 50 percent of the commercial houses in Mexico City, although Europeans only comprised 2 percent of the population. On the other hand, the creoles who comprised 49 percent of the population were able to control the other 50 percent of the mercantile firms.[24] It was largely the castas who were left out of the mercantile professions, except in rare cases.

The wealthier merchants hoarded most of the viceroyalty's silver coinage in order to ensure their dominance of the business with the incoming fleets. Increasingly, during the eighteenth century, this practice accentuated Mexico's shortage of currency because New Spain had no bank notes. The inevitable result was that both petty trader and almacenero (large-scale merchant) were forced to conduct the majority of their business on credit. The most popular device used in the eighteenth century was a bill-of-exchange called a libranza.[25]

The Jesuits were the initial users of libranzas, facilitating the purchase of essential goods from Mexico City merchants for interior estates (haciendas). Following the expulsion of the Jesuits in 1767, the Conde de Regla, Don Romero de Terreros, continued to redeem these instruments of credit.[26] After the adoption of comercio libre, with the increased volume in industry, trade, and agriculture, the libranza gained wider usage as an acceptable substitute for currency by the more established mercantile firms associated with the Mexico City consulado.

The consulado was an institution established to oversee the commercial networks of New Spain. In particular, the Tribunal del Real Consulado was the chief judicial organ to deal with commercial litigation. The Mexico City consulado was created in 1595 to augment those of the peninsula located in Sevilla and Cádiz. With the monopolistic control of trade by Sevilla and Cádiz, the Mexican consulado was unable to assert itself until the eighteenth century. Approximately half of the membership of the Mexican consulado resided in Mexico City. Of this half, 87.9 percent had been born in Spain, largely in the north. The two factions which struggled for dominance of this institution, the montañeses and vizcaínos were both peninsular in their composition.[27]

In 1793 Revillagigedo reported that the prestigious Mexico City consulado had opposed the introduction of <u>comercio libre</u>. The viceroy noted that the Mexico City consulado was an obstacle to the process of commercial liberalization. Because this body desired a monopolized marketplace, the membership placed little value on any economic development except their own. The Mexican consuladp made litigants travel long distances on poor roads to clear up their cases, most notably the merchants of Veracruz and Guadalajara. Revillagigedo's main complaint against the consulado, however, was that it served its own interests to the detriment of the other merchants of the viceroyalty.[28]

The institutional corollary to the incorporation of New Spain into <u>comercio libre</u> in 1789 was the creation of two consulados in 1795. On 17 January 1795, under a <u>real cédula</u>, the viceroy granted to Veracruz a license to create a new consulado.[29] The other Mexican city allowed to establish its own consulado was that of Guadalajara. The Guadalajaran consulado was authorized by a <u>real cédula</u> issued 8 June 1795.[30] Both consulados were founded to enhance commercial activities by ending the virtual monopoly which the Mexico City consulado tried to maintain. The primary purpose of the Veracruz consulado was to aid in the development of trade. In addition, the consulado was charged with promoting agriculture. The advancement in agriculture was expected to be accomplished through an improvement in cultivation techniques, the introduction of new technology (machinery), new implements, and the expansion of areas under cultivation. Both the Veracruz and the Guadalajara consulados were instructed in their respective charters to construct roads and bridges. Specifically, the Veracruz consulado became involved in the construction of the road from Veracruz to Mexico City by completing the link between Jalapa and Veracruz.[31]

The Mexican consulado was not pleased with the creation of these competitive bodies housed in Veracruz and Guadalajara. From the beginning, the Mexico City merchants undertook a campaign to discredit both of these bodies. Using the nobility within its ranks, the Mexican consulado merchants continually bombarded the viceregal government during the 1790s and early 1800s with petitions to extinguish these bodies.

In September 1796, Viceroy Branciforte sent a letter to Manuel de Godoy citing support for the abolition of the Veracruz and Guadalajara consulados. Branciforte noted that the Mexican consulado had a long term commitment to public works, such as the construction of the Veracruz-Mexico City highway. Branciforte also reported that the expenses incurred to run the three consulados were large, and that duties on goods rose to 15 percent in order to finance these bodies. He called, therefore, for the immediate disestablishment of the Veracruz and Guadalajara consulados.[32] Branciforte's proposal was ignored by the government in Madrid. The Mexican consulado continued to press for the suppression of the other two consulados until the beginning of the War of Independence. Little data exists to confirm whether the Veracruz and Guadalajara consulados were detrimental or of great benefit to the commerce.

An important function of the viceregal government was the promotion of domestic and international commerce. Viceroy Revillagigedo was an especially aggressive advocate of commercial expansion. In 1791 he drafted a model set of ordinances for the administration of the _Mercado de Volador_ (a marketplace) in Mexico City. This action was prompted by Revillagigedo's decision in 1789 to suppress sidewalk sales, the viceroy believing that sidewalk sales spurred vagrancy and criminal activity.[33]

The 1791 ordinances which governed the _Mercado de Volador_ organized the marketplace into 303 closed stalls to house the wares of the merchants. Stall numbers 1 to 24 were reserved for the sale of cloth products, such as raw cloth, hats, and mantles. These articles were principally made from cotton. Stalls numbered between 25 and 48 were reserved for sales of candy, dried fruits, cheese, butter, eggs, chile, and other agricultural commodities. These retail shops were permanent structures. Some of the other stalls were temporary installations.

Other permanent structures located in the *Mercado de Volador* were reserved for the sale of manufactured or semi-industrial products. Stalls numbered 49 through 72 sold iron and copper horseshoes. Shops 169 through 192 sold chinaware, cured leather, shoes, furniture, and other similar manufactured products.[34] Some stalls were assigned to the sale of foodstuffs. Retail shops numbered 97 to 144 sold primarily domestic fruits. Stalls 145 through 168 sold fresh meats and fish. Finally, the stalls numbered between 194 and 303 were reserved for the sale of corn and wheat which the Indians brought into the city.

The ordinances drafted by Revillagigedo included clauses which set up a *juez de plaza*, an inspector who settled minor disputes. His salary was twelve hundred pesos per annum. Included in the administration of the market was a manager called an *administrador*, who saw that the streets were kept clean and lighted at night. This manager was additionally responsible for procuring sufficient amounts of fuel oil for the street-lamps and hiring the personnel to maintain them. Normally, the *administrador* employed two *guardaministros* to attend to these tasks.[35]

These retail shops in the *Mercado de Volador* were not free to the merchants who utilized them. The *almaceneros* were required to pay rent. The rent paid ranged from eighteen reales to forty-two reales per week, depending upon the location of the stall. The normal range for rental of a stall was somewhere between twenty-nine and thirty-six reales weekly. The rent concept was incorporated into the 1791 ordinances in order to provide funds to maintain the condition of the marketplace and expand operations. In addition, shopkeepers were required to pay between one and three reales per month for the street-light outside their stores.[36]

The Reglamento para los mercados de México drafted by Revillagigedo in 1791 became the main ordinance for local commerce in urban centers and were utilized throughout New Spain by the second decade of the nineteenth century. Revillagigedo claimed in his 1794 Instruccion reservada that the primary focus of the 1791 ordinances had been to reorganize all of Mexico's marketplaces.[37] Viceroy Azanza reported in 1800 that the reforms instituted by Revillagigedo had succeeded in increasing commerce in the Mexican marketplaces. He wanted to require that all retail shops be reconstructed of a more durable material; wood was not fire resistant.[38] In general, the local marketplace was the most important vehicle for internal commerce.

The crown for its part in promoting commerce and industry offered an unusual proposal toward the end of the eighteenth century. In 1790 the crown proposed the establishment of a Royal Maritime Company that would promote international commerce between Spain and her colonies. Revillagigedo was not entirely receptive to this idea. He believed that this company would further monopolize transatlantic commerce.[39]

Probably the most interesting idea to foster commercial expansion came from Vicente Basadre in 1807. Basadre, formerly the secretary of the consulado of Veracruz, noted that the technical knowledge of the average merchant was low. Most merchants learned about the technical aspects of commercial activity through a trial and error process. Basadre therefore advocated the establishment of special academies which would educate potential merchants. He believed that such institutions would improve the quality of the average merchant and thereby foster commercial development. Basadre also expressed the opinion that many unsavory merchants or persons could be excluded from these academies. The principal participants in these schools would be members of the upper and middle classes.[40]

The chief institutional body within the viceregal government which dealt with both internal and external commerce was the <u>Real Aduana</u> (Royal customhouse). This subagency of the Royal Exchequer gained added strength after the promulgation of the intendant ordinances in 1786. Customhouses were located in all the important cities of New Spain.[41] During the late eighteenth century, the number of customhouse officials increased because of the expanded commercial activities in New Spain. Between 1754 and 1789, the number of customs officials grew from 88 to 125. The most important customhouses servicing New Spain's international trade were those in Veracruz and Acapulco.[42]

Mexican international trade was a primary beneficiary of the introduction of *comercio libre*. By the end of the eighteenth century, duties on international trade had been severely curtailed or reduced. In 1800 the average master of a ship entering Veracruz paid a wide range of duties, depending upon where his ship was registered. A ship entering Veracruz from a European port paid a 3 percent *almojarifazgo* and a 5 percent alcabala. With the Peace of Amiens in 1802 the alcabala duty was reduced to 3 percent.[43]

Duties for ships entering Veracruz from or via other Indies ports were much higher. Prior to 1804 each ship arriving in Veracruz from an Indies port paid a 5 percent alcabala and a 7 percent *almojarifazgo*. After 1804 the alcabala duty was lowered to 3 percent. The *almojarifazgo* for ships from Indies ports remained at 7 percent. Goods transported from Veracruz overland were charged a 3 percent alcabala. Ships leaving Veracruz destined for other Indies seaports only paid a 4 percent *derecho de salida* (departure duty).[44]

The era following the adoption of *comercio libre* witnessed a phenomenal growth in the international trade of New Spain. In 1792 the total importation into Veracruz was valued at 8.8 million pesos and total exportation at 12.7 million pesos. Thus the value of the trade conducted through the port of Veracruz was 21.5 million pesos in 1792. The amount of Spanish goods entering Veracruz in 1792 was 5.5 million pesos. Only 3.3 million pesos in foreign goods, however, entered Mexico through the seaport of Veracruz. The statistics for 1792 confirm the continued importance of silver in the international trade of New Spain. More than 8.9 million pesos in silver bullion was transported to Spain, constituting the largest single component of Veracruz's seaborne trade with the mother country. Other commodities were shipped to Spain via Veracruz and their value in 1792 was 3.8 million pesos.[45] In the decade between 1792 and 1802, the total amount of commercial traffic flowing through Veracruz was valued at 60.3 million pesos. Exports from Veracruz were 38.4 million pesos including silver bullion. Total value of imports which entered Mexico via Veracruz in 1802 was 21.9 million pesos.[46]

Economic statistics of the late colonial era indicate that precious metals dominated the international trade of New Spain. Between 1796 and 1813, more than 138 million pesos of silver and gold bullion were transported from Veracruz to Spain. In comparison, the export commodity coming nearest silver in importance was cochineal. Between 1796 and 1813 more than 22.6 million pesos of cochineal was shipped to Spain via Veracruz. Sugar exportation in the same era was only 8.2 million pesos. Clearly, between 1796 and 1813 precious metals constituted the principal item of Mexico's commerce.[47]

During the late eighteenth century, the viceroys attempted to expand both international and domestic trade. The Bourbon crown focused its program upon increasing the trade between Spain and the Indies. The primary institution for commercial interaction before Mexico's inclusion into the regime of comercio libre was the trade fair. After the implementation of comercio libre in 1789, trading activity was based more on individual accomplishment. Most merchants traded their wares in the large urban markets where demand was greatest. Free trade shifted the primary concern of the viceroys toward reforming local commerce and increasing competition among the Mexican merchant elite. Revillagigedo's 1791 ordinances dealing with standardizing local marketplaces and their operations can be viewed as a major viceregal commercial reform in the late eighteenth century. Establishment of the consulados of Guadalajara and Veracruz in 1795 resulted in more competition among the merchant elite. Revillagigedo had spurred this action because of his recurrent criticisms of the economic power of the merchants associated with the Mexico City consulado. The most important commercial reform of the eighteenth century was comercio libre. Most viceregal programs were designed to augment this basic Bourbon policy change.

CHAPTER VI

GOVERNMENT AND SOCIETY

The Spanish Bourbons inherited a chaotic and devastated Spanish peninsula in 1700. For nearly a century Spain had undergone a decline in both its wealth and status in the world community.[1] From the outset of their rule on the peninsula, the Bourbons attributed Spain's economic and political decay to Hapsburg misrule. Phillip V assumed the Spanish throne and thereupon decided to "reform" Spain and her colonial possessions. He was accompanied to Spain with French bureaucrats who were cognizant of the great strides made in reforming France's own decaying political and economic system.[2] Almost immediately the new Bourbon monarch introduced the French intendant system to the Spanish peninsula. The intendant system succeeded in arresting the economic and political chaos in Spain as a consequence of Hapsburg neglect and the War of the Spanish Succession. After some years the crown and its advisers began to reassess the system which governed the Spanish Indies. In 1743, José Campillo y Cosío's _Nuevo sistema de gobierno económico para la América_ was presented to the king, Phillip V. This book circulated among the officialdom of Spain until its publication in 1789.[3]

Campillo's Nuevo sistema became the focal point of the reforms which ensued in the Spanish Indies during the eighteenth century. Within this work was a recommendation that independent intendancies be established in the Indies. In reality, by the 1760s intendancies were the cornerstone of Spanish imperial politics. They would become the quintessence of the patrimonial state. For nearly a century the Hapsburg monarchs had allowed their government to be corrupted. Public offices, both in Spain and the Indies, were sold with little thought as to the competence of the individuals filling high government posts. Graft and corruption thereby was rampant in the Spanish Indies.[4] The colonists, however, opposed the institution of the intendancies. Because of the decline of royal authority during the latter stages of the seventeenth century, many colonists had gained government positions and great wealth. Centralization into the hands of crown sponsored intendants would and did result in their decline.[5]

Spain's continuing rivalry with Great Britain in the eighteenth century moreover delayed the implementation of these reforms advocated by Campillo and many others within the Spanish government. Beginning in 1757 the Bourbons became embroiled in a war with Great Britain on the side of France, which was later called the Seven Years War. The capture of Cuba in 1762 both shocked and alarmed the Spanish government. Their new monarch was Charles III, who showed few signs of greatness at the outset of his reign, decided to reassess Spanish strengths and weaknesses. For him the defeats suffered at the hands of the British became a turning-point in his reign. After signing the humiliating Treaty of Paris in 1763, Charles began to review the whole structure of colonial government.[6] In 1765 he dispatched one of his ablest advisers, José de Gálvez, to the Kingdom of New Spain; the pearl of the Spanish empire. As with all of the reforms initiated in late Bourbon Mexico, they begin with the epic and famous Gálvez Visitation (1765-1771).[7]

Gálvez arrived in New Spain during late 1765 and thereupon made his way to the capital of the viceroyalty, Mexico City. His entrance into the capital was not greeted with much fanfare. Within a short time relations between Gálvez and the viceroy, the Marqués de Cruillas, deteriorated as a consequence of the visitador's zeal and reforms. He also helped in the expulsion of the Jesuits which gained him the emnity of the populace. He reformed the tobacco monopoly over the protestations of its head, Don Juan Antonio Velarde. Both of these events are well known to all students of Mexican history.[8] But that which concerns us here are the reforms which engendered consternation among the largely creole based oligarchy and bureaucracy. In essence, Gálvez was in a vanguard of a revolution in government which assisted in the growth of the patrimonial state--an event which forever changed the course of Mexican history.

Gálvez was sent to Bourbon Mexico with one goal in mind--to regain Spanish hegemony. By the early decades of the 1700s most lower level positions in the colonial government were held by creoles. Gálvez was instructed to replace them with a cadre of officials sent from Europe. Bitterness soon pervaded the viceregal government of New Spain. Both the audiencia of Mexico City and Church officials were critical of this move by Gálvez who acted in the king's name. Presumably Gálvez was given these instructions before he left Bourbon Spain. Many governorships and capitanias-generales, held by Mexican creoles, were soon replaced with Spaniards and especially militarymen. Gálvez was critical of the increased creole presence within the colonial government and adamant about replacing them with Spaniards. The future Minister of the Indies claimed that "these men were too bound by the ties of family and faction...to provide a disinterested impartial government."[9] Gálvez was appalled that most oidor positions in the audiencia of Mexico City were retained by creoles. Such an occurrence harmed and diminished the authority of the monarchy.[10] Indeed, throughout the New World Gálvez found creoles dominating their political setting.

Galvez pondered as to the best means in arresting or curtailing this increasing presence of Americans in colonial government. Eventually he agreed with officials in Madrid that the only effective means to ending creole dominance was that of instituting an intendancy program. In January 1768 Gálvez completed his first intendancy plan for New Spain.[11] This is a rather detailed explanation of the reasons or necessity to establish intendancies in Bourbon Mexico. Chief among the reasons for implementing such government entities in the New World, Galvez observed, was their success in the Iberian peninsula. The *visitador* found that confusion was rampant within the structure of the government of New Spain. Local political or civil bodies often duplicated the activities borne by the viceregal government. It is clear that Gálvez's motive for proposing intendancies was that of strengthening Spanish rule in Mexico.[12] These plans were in addition blueprints for a strengthened patrimonial state. Creole influence was too great according to the Gálvez view.

A major part of Gálvez's plan deals with the finances of the realm and consequently with the economy. The *visitador* observed that the officialdom of New Spain was plagued with corruption, particularly at the level of the *alcaldes mayores* and *corregidores*. Gálvez therefore reasoned that a centralized and efficient body, such as the intendants, would decrease the graft and corruption existing in Bourbon Mexico. One of the more important facets of the Gálvez plan involved the administration of the Royal Exchequer or *Real Hacienda*. His plan called for an increased role for exchequer officials. Henceforth it would have a center stage role in the society of the Mexican colony. Gálvez called for an enlarged bureaucracy, under the auspices of the *Real aduana*, to collect the taxes and duties due the Spanish crown. Such a plan appealed to Charles III and officials in Madrid.[13]

The response to the Gálvez plan was not immediate. While in New Spain the future Minister of the Indies had made a number of enemies both in Spain and the New World. In Spain, the Council of the Indies feared the growing power and influence of the *visitador*. This body was concerned about the plan because he had not consulted them before making these proposals. In New Spain, once his plan became generally known to the officialdom, they believed him to have a sinister intent--to deny creoles of their rightful positions within the colonial government. Resentment toward Gálvez and his plan thus tempered royal action.[14] Gálvez returned to Spain in 1771 without realizing his goal of placing intendants in Bourbon Mexico. His power and prestige, however, had grown as a consequence of his exploits in the New World. Within the king's innercircle he continued to clamor for reform.

In 1776 Gálvez was named the Minister of the Indies by Charles III. Almost immediately he began to move. First, he installed intendants in the viceroyalty of the Río de la Plata and then in Peru as well.[15] Neither did the minister abandon his plans for New Spain. In August

1779 Don Pedro Antonio de Cossío was named superintendant of the Royal Exchequer.[16] This action became the prelude to the introduction of intendants into Bourbon Mexico. It is clear that the chief purpose in naming a financial superintendant was to improve the finances of the crown and of the viceregal government as well. A byproduct of this action was to create resentment among the colonial elites who worried that this step would lead to a total domination of the Mexican economy. And once the intendants were dispatched to the Mexican colony they did become the chief administrators of economic affairs and consequently helped nuture the development of the patrimonial state. Gálvez, as Minister of the Indies, continued to lobby for the establishment of intendants in the Mexican viceroyalty. Finally in 1786, Charles III authorized the introduction of intendants into New Spain. Gálvez had achieved his long soughtafter goal, however, not with a great deal of sacrifice and work between 1776 and 1786.[17]

In Bourbon Mexico, Gálvez's plan got off to a slow start in comparison to Peru and the Río de la Plata. While he had drained the viceroy of many of his former power, he still remained at the head of the viceregal government. In the case of Cossío, failure followed him throughout his lackluster career. Cossío, as superintendant of the Royal Exchequer, tried to gain total control over the Real aduana. But opposition soon surfaced in reaction to his attempted takeover and eventually Cossío received a reprimand from Madrid. Officials in Spain claimed he had exceeded his authority. Between 1779 and 1782 he tried to impose a centralized bureaucratic structure over finances but with little success.[18] Ultimately Cossío was dismissed from service because of his excesses. The death of the two succeeding viceroys, Matías and Bernardo de Gálvez, also impeded the transition to the intendant system in New Spain. In December 1786, Charles III finally agreed with Gálvez and authorized the promulgation of the ordenanzas de intendentes for New Spain.[19] Thereafter Bourbon Mexico was divided into twelve intendancies. They consisted of the provinces of Yucatan, Oaxaca, Puebla, México, Veracruz, Valladolid, Guanajuato, Guadalajara, Zacatecas, Durango, San Luís Potosí, and Sonora.

Gálvez, who was responsible for the promulgation of the intendant decree, was given the authority to appoint the men who would serve in these positions. Each province received an intendant as well as a legal aide and lieutenant. Gálvez was not sympathetic to the creole cause and except for one post, all of the intendants named were Spaniards. The Minister of the Indies had a deep seated contempt for creole society and consequently was a prime advocate of Spanish-Patrimonialism in Mexico.[20]

Most of the intendant appointees were chosen from the Gálvez lineage as well as trusted friends and allies of the minister. To oversee the intendants he appointed Don Fernando Mangiño as the superintendente subdelegado de real hacienda. Mangiño had been one of Galvez's most trusted friends since the days of the visitation. Of the twelve men chosen by Gálvez; five were from the military services, four had been revenue officials, and at least four were relatives of the minister.[21]

The establishment of the intendancies in New Spain during 1786 changed the nature of politics in the Mexican colony. As chart 1 illustrates, the intendant ordinances made the revenue officials much more important within the Mexican setting. For this reason, the Mexican economy became increasingly patrimonial in character, particularly in its administration. In reality the intendant became the chief economic agent in each intendancy. He headed the four dominant estates of government. They were delineated as follows: Justice, War, Exchequer, and *Policia*.[22] Of crucial importance to the present discussion, the intendant had greater powers than any other official in colonial Mexican history. In the area of fiscal administration the intendant had no rivals. Upon the promulgation of the *ordenanzas*, responsibility for the collection of duties and taxes passed into the hands of the intendants. Previous to this date local authorities

CHART 1

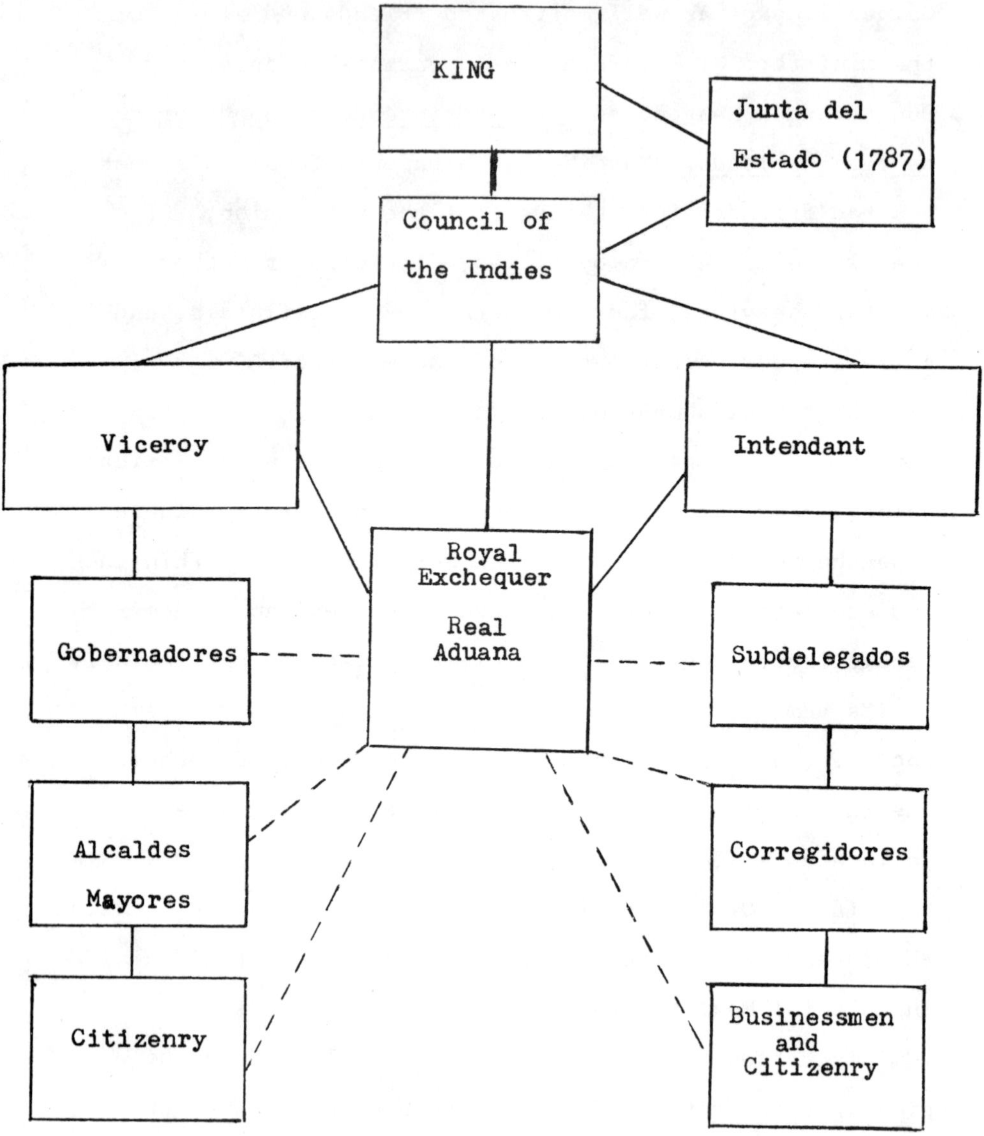

BUREAUCRATIC-PATRIMONIALISM IN NEW SPAIN

could remit their receipts to Mexico City. Now the crown set up regional treasuries to house the revenues collected by the intendants and their subordinates. To ensure their dominance in the Mexican setting, Gálvez gave them an indeterminate appointment. In essence, they could serve as long as they were successful.[23] Several of the intendants appointed in 1786 continued to serve in Bourbon Mexico until 1810.

For a time Gálvez continued to pursue his progam of diminishing viceregal authority. To this end he placed Ferando Mangiño in the post of superintendente subdelegado de real hacienda; which was totally independent of viceregal authority. Mangiño, however, quarrelled bitterly with the viceroy and other officials. But more importantly, in 1787, his chief benefactor, Gálvez, was replaced as Minister of the Indies. Frey Antonio Valdés y Bazan assumed Galvez's ministerial post in 1787 and thereupon decided to discard the superintendente subdelegado as an independent position. This former office was consequently reunited to the viceroy. Mangiño departed from Bourbon Mexico and was appointed to the prestigious Council of the Indies.[24] With the removal of the superintendente subdelegado position from the Mexican setting, central authority for intendancy affairs shifted to the junta superior de real hacienda. This body differed markedly from the superintendente subdelegado. Whereas the superintendent was all powerful, the viceroy acted merely as chairman of the *junta superior*. The *junta superior* thereby made all of the decisions regarding intendancy affairs.[25] In essence, this new bureaucracy directed all intendancy operations and even adjudicated all conflicts involving intendants in exchequer affairs. This decentralized body, although active, ultimately lacked conviction in the purpose of the ordinances. They acted more in accord with the interests of the colony than those in Madrid.

In 1789 Charles IV appointed one of its ardent supporters, the Second Conde de Revillagigedo, as viceroy of New Spain. From the outset of his viceregency he attacked the *junta superior* as a "corrupt and useless body." He found their meetings rather boring and in accord with the vices of the old order.[26] He called for the abolition of this body. In 1791 Revillagigedo complained about the abuses of the *alcaldes mayores*. Even after the promulgation of the intendant ordinances in 1786, graft and corruption pervaded the activities borne by the *alcaldes*. They continued to engage in trade; strictly forbidden by the ordinances.[27] However, Revillagigedo could not succeed in obtaining higher salaries for the subdelegates. He believed that such an occurrence would relieve them of the need to engage in trade. But no authorization was forwarded and the subdelegates as a consequence continued to engage in commerce in contravention of the intendant ordinances.

By 1794 Viceroy Revillagigedo was no longer as supportive of the intendant scheme as he had been when he assumed his viceregency. In his Instrucción reservada of 1794, the enlightened viceroy indicated that little had been gained by the intendant reforms beyond the increased power of the Bourbon monarchy.[28]

Whatever else is true about the intendancy system of New Spain, the intendants had clearly become the chief administrators within the Mexican economy. Viceroy Revillagigedo increased their role in directing the Mexican economy. Throughout his viceregency he encouraged them to promote economic development. The revenue hungry government of late Bourbon Mexico needed an ever increasing supply of funds to sustain its activities and to pay the salaries of the burgeoning royal bureaucracy.[29] During Revillagigedo's viceregency the role of the intendants in economic affairs both grew and intensified. In 1791 the viceroy issued an order calling upon the intendants to draft detailed reports concerning the principal economic pursuits in their respective provinces. These reports, created under the auspices of the Conde de Revillagigedo, are probably the best and most accurate of the late colonial period.[30] Among those who reported to the viceroy were Manuel de Flon, Antonio de Mora y Peysar, Phelipe Díaz de Hortega, Bruno Díaz de Salcedo, Josef de Peón Valdés,

Juan Antonio de Riaño, and José Fernando de Abascal y Sousa.[31] All of these reports note the principal industries found in the intendancies; the existence of infrastructure such as roads, bridges, seaports, and canals. For the most part they recounted that agriculture was the dominant activity among the Mexican populace and only the provincial capitals evidenced any degree of industrialization beyond craft industries.[32]

Bureaucrats by the late eighteenth century were essential to the smooth running of the Mexican viceroyalty and patrimonial state. The patrimonial state, with its hordes of functionaries, needed an ever increasing financial base to keep it operating. During the period after 1786 treasuries were placed in all important sites of trade and industry. Relationships between businessmen and bureaucrats changed. Many career bureaucrats married into the prominent merchant families.[33] New Spain, by 1800, had truely become a colonial society. It was a creole society dominated by hacendados, merchants, and miners. The intendants thus served as the intermediaries between the society at large and the patrimonial state. Graft and corruption was not ended with the appointment of intendants in the late Mexican colony. But these vices were less apparent, at least to officials in Madrid and Mexico City. Their appearance from Spain made them foreigners even among the creole oligarchy.

Indeed, the intendants, because of their actions, often created friction between the viceregal government and the bulk of Mexican society. Because of the large volume of work, few intendants ever ventured outside of their provincial capital. The intendants consequently relied on the local, largely creole, bureaucracy to fulfill their duties in the hinterlands.[34]

By 1794 Viceroy Revillagigedo was no longer as ardent in his support for the intendants. In his mind, they had failed to end the practice of allowing subdelegates to extract a portion of the Indians' tribute payments. This abuse the viceroy attributed to the misdeeds and mismanagement of the Council of the Indies. Revillagigedo had been appointed viceroy of New Spain, in part, because of his zeal for the Bourbon reforms and because of his administrative abilities. Throughout his viceregency he tried to achieve the aims of the Spanish crown. Of note, he was an enthusiastic supporter of comercio libre, which he claimed did much to improve the economic conditions prevalent in late Bourbon Mexico. Revillagigedo, however, realized that one sole policy was not sufficient to reform the Mexican economy. He was an advocate of centralized power in the hands of a bureaucratic elite. From the ouset of his viceregency, he quarrelled with the creole elite. He saw them as instruments of local creole power rather then being supporters of royalist power. The creole elite, on the other hand, saw the viceroy as a usuper of their privileges.[35]

Revillagigedo was clearly an advocate of political change in late Bourbon Mexico. He saw the colonial elite as rival to regalist power. To curb their influence within the Mexican colony he made a series of proposals between 1790 and 1794. Among them, he advocated the creation of more <u>consulados</u> and <u>gremios</u>. Revillagigedo believed that these additional corporate bodies would encourage competition and thereby give the crown more power. We may view the intendants as an extension of this idea. Previously the colonial officialdom had lacked effective power to curb the excesses of the dominant elites. In essence, Revillagigedo's disdain and distrust of the creole classes emanated from the officialdom in Madrid which considered colonial subjects as inferior. Throughout his viceregency he showed contempt for creole society. His subsequent successors, the Marqués de Branciforte and Miguel José de Azanza, were not much different in their attitudes toward this colonial society.[36]

By the late colonial period, Mexico was a land of ethnic contrasts. As of 1804 the European element comprised less than two percent of the population. Power, however, resided in their hands. Through Spanish born intendants, this group controlled the political and economic life of the viceroyalty. New Spain by independence had become essentially a patrimonial state which adhered to the Bourbon precepts concerning an orderly society. True, the creoles dominated the lesser provincial offices and more importantly the mercantile firms of late Bourbon Mexico. Yet as of 1804 the creoles (white Americans) only comprised little more than sixteen percent of the population.[37] What was the real difference between Spanish or creole rule? The answer is evident. For the bulk of the Mexican populace, who belonged to the castas, there was little difference who ruled Mexico. While the Hidalgo and Morelos revolts reflected the aspirations of the disenfranchised castas, the Mexican Wars of Independence became a classical war between two oligarchies.

In reality, the Wars of Independence were just a transition to creole rule. Few rewards came to the mestizos and castes of Mexico after the Spaniards departed. Independence led to philosophical and political conflict between the creoles and their leaders. Some supported centralism while others supported federalism. Until the dictatorship of Porfirio Díaz, Mexico was consumed with recurrent internal strife over what form of government would rule Mexico. Díaz, in essence, returned Mexico to its heritage. He chose to return to the patrimonial state. It became a state which served the ends of the creole elite in the name of economic development and modernization. The Mexican Revolution, on the other hand, became a catalyst for social change. Creole rule was ended and in its place arose mestizo rule. But here again we must be careful in describing this development as mass rule, for this would be untrue. The ultimate outcome was a compromise between the creole and mestizo elites. The Partido Revolucionario Institucional (PRI) is the embodiment of this compromise. Since the 1918 Constitution was promulgated the Mexican state and in particular the Mexican economy has been governed by a patrimonial state. Rewards were distributed to those who supported this state and aims of the PRI. Who is to say that this is not proper? The patrimonial state reflects a continuity in Mexican history. It provides a strong central government which can promote economic development and at the same time protect the state from possible insurrection or rebellion.

CHAPTER VII

BUREAUCRACY AND FINANCIAL MANAGEMENT

Finances were an integral part of the patrimonial economy of late Bourbon Mexico. With the advent of Charles III's rule in 1759, efficiency in government became a primary objective of colonial bureaucrats. Revenue consequently became of increased importance and significance to fund and extend the bureaucratic state in Spanish Mexico. Charles III and his ministers believed in a much more centralized form of government. The Hapsburgs in comparison had allowed a greater degree of autonomy in the operation of government in the Mexican colony.[1] Essentially, in the first phase of the Caroline economic reforms, colonial officials were charged with promoting and increasing the powers of the regalist state. Because Spanish Mexico was the most important realm in the New World, particular attention was placed on centralizing its economy. All sectors of this economy, under Bourbon rule, were reorganized so that the crown and its colonial officialdom, most notably the viceroys and intendants, played a pivotal role in its administration and development. The Bourbon reformers knew and believed that increased economic activity meant increased revenues in the crown's coffers. Bourbon rule consequently also signaled an increased and expanded role for the Royal Exchequer and its subsidiaries.[2] Bureaucrats played an important if not essential role in the financial well-being of late Bourbon Mexico.

Fiscal conditions both in Spain and the Indies improved in the late colonial era. The revitalization of the mining industry seems to be the most immediate reason for this rebound, particularly in Bourbon Mexico. Zacatecas and Guanajuato were the chief mining regions in late colonial Mexico and it was their revitalization which gave new life to the Mexican economy.[3] This improved economic climate, however, was not limited only to the mining sector. Indeed, agriculture and transatlantic trade, as evidenced in the preceding chapters, also expanded markedly during this epoch. As a consequence the coffers of the colonial government received more revenues. Such developments in New Spain were greeted with joy by the Caroline reformers in Madrid. The expansion of the economy of Spanish Mexico now took on new significance. Caroline economic thought now took firm hold within the Spanish ministries and likewise among the officialdom in Bourbon Mexico. The mercantilism advocated by the Physiocrats became a reality both in Spain and the Mexican colony. A cornerstone of the economic reforms and economic expansion of the late eighteenth century was the patrimonial state.

As with the other reforms undertaken in New Spain during the late eighteenth century, their birth is linked to the Gálvez Visitation. Gálvez arrived in Mexico during 1765 and immediately noticed the fiscal chaos existing in this New World colony. From the outset he believed that centralization was the key to improving colonial administration. Among his first actions after his entrance into Mexico City was that of reforming the Royal Exchequer. In his informe, which he forwarded to Charles III, he advocated an expansion of this colonial service. More revenue agents, he concluded, should be employed by the crown to increase the funds due the king. Key among these were taxes collected from the monopolies created after 1764. In addition, Gálvez advocated an expanded aduana (customs agency) to meet the ever increasing sums emanating from trade and commerce. All of these steps he reasoned were necessary to end the fiscal-administrative problems existing in late colonial Mexico.[4]

The Gálvez proposals were subsequently scrutinized by officials in Madrid. Many were acted on, however, not to the degree that he had hoped for or envisioned. The Conde de Aranda and other officials in the Caroline court were cognizant of the unrest they might cause if they were embraced completely. Beginning in 1766 Charles III authorized Viceroy Francisco de Croix to increase the number of revenue officials in New Spain. To improve the productivity of the Royal Exchequer, the crown called for the construction of additional customhouses. Previously, all revenues collected in the Mexican colony were shipped to Mexico City.[5] Such a practice delayed the receipt of income and consequently impinged on the delivery of surpluses to the king's coffers in Spain. Between 1760 and 1789 the revenues of Bourbon Mexico grew some four fold. However, after 1789 the Mexican economy took a decided spurt forward.[6]

With the entrance of Viceroy Revillagigedo into New Spain during the 1790s the role of government changed and intensified. He is the starkest advocate of the patrimonial state during the late colonial period. He was also the man who implemented the intendancy reforms. Throughout his viceregency he called for an "enlightened" approach to colonial administration. He was a proponent of the peninsularization of the Mexican bureaucracy. Revillagigedo, from the beginning of his administration, believed in his mission of making New Spain a resource to the Spanish crown. Upon entering New Spain the intendancies produced some 50 million pesos in revenues. For the year of 1789 when this budget was calculated we find that the total expenditures of the viceregal government amounted to only 38 million pesos. This left New Spain with a surplus of some 12 million pesos.[7] These figures illustrate the relative strength of the Mexican economy. Revillagigedo's estimates indicate how successful the bureaucracy was in the collection of taxes. By the 1790s Bourbon Mexico was the most self-sufficient in the New World. With this success the patrimonial state grew and gained prominence. Finances consequently were the cornerstone of the Bourbon reformers attempts to promote and expand royal power.

Of great importance to the development of the state in late colonial Mexico were the reforms associated with the aduana. In the aftermath of the Galvez Visitation, the aduana was expanded tremendously. This agency was deemed essential to spur the income generated from commerce. As stated previously, new customhouses were emplaced in Puebla, Oaxaca, Tlaxcala, Querétaro, Tepeaca, Tabasco, Toluca, Celaya, Guanajuato, Guadalajara, León, Cuernavaca, Zacatecas, Cordoba, Orizaba, Valladolid, San Miguel el Grande, San Luís Potosí, Durango, Jalapa, Chiguagua, Bolaños, Zimapán, and Pachuca. This expansive list illustrates just how extensive was this undertaking by the Royal Exchequer during the late colonial period.[8] In the aftermath of the introduction of intendants to New Spain, Viceroy Revillagigedo requested assistance from Don Miguel del Corral, Director of the Royal Corps of Engineers. The viceroy decided to redesign the customhouses found throughout the Mexican colony. Henceforth all of the customhouses would resemble the one located in Mexico City. In 1791 work began on the customhouses of Zacatecas and Guanajuato. Revillagigedo thought that they should receive a facelift before all others because of their importance as New Spain's chief mining areas.[9]

To man these customhouses the viceroyalty had a large cadre of officials. By 1791 each customhouse had at least a commander, a second lieutenant, and a larger number of lower level functionaries. The salary for the head of the customhouse ranged between 500 and 1200 pesos per annum. Quite naturally the more prestigious places paid more. Mexico City paid more than any other customhouse in Spanish Mexico. Expenditures in operating these economic way stations varied considerably from one location to another. Mexico City, for instance, had expenditures of 38,730 pesos in 1790 whereas the customhouse of Queretaro only recorded 4,575 pesos in the same year. The records of the _Real aduana_ of New Spain reveal that most expenditures went for the salaries and wages of the personnel to operate Mexico's many customhouses. Each bureaucracy had a particular mission to fulfill in late colonial Mexico and in the case of the _Real aduana_ their specific duty was that of collecting sales taxes (_alcabalas_), duties from seaborne commerce, and the taxes borne in the pulque trade.[10]

As stated previously in this monograph, the extensive nature of Mexican trade by the late eighteenth century necessitated a greatly expanded bureaucracy. This is especially true with regard to the Real aduana. When Gálvez submitted his report to the Council of the Indies in 1771, he found that New Spain had some 150 customs officials. Table 7 shows that the Real aduana grew markedly in the aftermath of the Gálvez Visitation.[11]

TABLE 7 PRINCIPAL CUSTOMHOUSES & PERSONNEL, 1790

Location	Number of Men
Mexico City	124
Puebla de los Angeles	33
Oaxaca	14
Tlaxcala	9
Querétaro	13
Tepeaca	13
Tabasco	3
Toluca	11
Celaya	18
Guanajuato	24
Guadalajara	29
León	10
Cuernavaca	3
Zacatecas	10
Córdoba	8
Orizaba	10
Valladolid	14
San Miguel el Grande	5
San Luís Potosí	7
Durango	7
Jalapa (Xalapa)	9
Chiguagua	1
Bolaños	3
Zimapán	2
Pachuca	1
Veracruz	42
Acapulco	33
TOTAL	492

SOURCE: MN, Reyno de México III, ms. 335.
NOTE: This list is not totally accurate. I could not locate personnel lists for all of the customhouses.

Even later in 1793 the Second Conde de Revillagigedo made note of the insufficient number of customs officials serving in the late Mexican colony. Such a circumstance the viceroy claimed was a detriment to the goals of the Bourbon monarchy and also to Mexican economic development.[12] Revenue officials thus were the premier officials within the colonial bureaucracy, especially after the promulgation of the intendant ordinances in 1786. Indeed, the superintendent of the Royal Exchequer wielded more power than the viceroy with regard to colonial finances and expenditures. As table 7 demonstrates the customhouses with the greatest number of officials indicate the most important economic centers found in the Mexican colony. It is only natural that those cities also had the largest revenues and thereby had greatest level of economic activity in the colony. Such an occurrence meant a great deal to an aspiring colonial bureaucracy. Customhouse income thus had an impact on the social order in late Bourbon Mexico. _Aduana_ officials competed for the wealthiest customhouses because they offered the greatest chance for upward social mobility. The _Real aduana_ of New was truely an instrument of patrimonial power. As a unit of the colonial government, it helped to control the Mexican economy. Officials both in Mexico City and Madrid used them to direct economic policies and therefore toward peninsular (Spanish) ends.[13]

The social composition of the *Real aduana* in the late Mexican colony also illustrates the nature and growth of the patrimonial state. As of 1790 all of the chief officers in New Spain's farflung customhouses were peninsulars. Roughly ninety percent of all of the positions in the *Real aduana* were held by persons from Spain. Creoles constituted the second tier or lower level in the customs agency. Most creoles filled positions such as scribe or guard. In this case, the guards protected the customhouse and assisted in the transport and collection of duties owed. This seems a bit surprising because the *Real aduana* was not a high status position for a peninsular.[14] By the late colonial period, however, the crown and its servants in the Mexican colony had embarked on a program of rapid centralization and peninsularization. Most historians point to the intendant reforms as the focal point of the administrative reforms enacted in the late colonial period. This interpretation, although accurate, fails to take into account the reforms performed on the much larger colonial bureaucracy. Indeed, the intendant reforms were a catalyst but the reform of finances took on a larger significance in the reform scheme of the Bourbon monarchy and its advisers in the Council of the Indies.

Any reform initiated in the late colonial epoch also bore costs as well. In the case of the *Real aduana*, expenditures rose as this colonial bureaucracy grew. Table 8 illustrates the extensive nature of the expenditures borne

TABLE 8 EXPENDITURES OF CUSTOMS COLLECTION, 1790

Location	Amount/Pesos
Mexico City	38,730
Puebla de los Angeles	12,415
Oaxaca	5,680
Tlaxcala	2,450
Querétaro	4,575
Tepeaca	2,650
Tabasco	1,050
Toluca	4,036
Celaya	1,224
Guanajuato	2,884
Guadalajara	9,073
León	2,575
Cuernavaca	32
Zacatecas	4,685
Córdoba	2,507
Orizaba	2,555
Valladolid	5,150
San Miguel el Grande	1,700
San Luís Potosí	2,790
Durango	2,295
Jalapa (Xalapa)	3,340
Chiguagua	500
Bolaños	1,700
Zimapán	416
Pachuca	300
Veracruz	9,683
Acapulco	8,495
TOTAL	133,490

SOURCE: MN, Reyno de México III, ms. 335.
NOTE: Statistics for Veracruz and Acapulco come from MN, Papeles Varios IV, ms. 317.

in 1790 to maintain the <u>Real aduana</u>. As of 1790 nearly 134 thousand pesos were paid out from the viceregal coffers to finance the expenses of the customs agency. Quite naturally, the capital of the viceroyalty, Mexico City, accounted for a lion share of the expenditures as compared to the other cities of late Bourbon Mexico. The great seaports of

Veracruz and Acapulco also had large expenditures because of their roles as entrepots of seaborne commerce. In fact, the expenditures for these three cities above amounted to nearly one-third of the total. We may surmise then that customs operations were rather brisk in these locations. Table 8 does not reflect where these expenditures were ultimately spent. From my research it would seem that the vast majority went to pay for the salaries and wages of the men serving the Real aduana in the late Mexican colony.[15] Salaries for the employees ranged between a mere thirty-two pesos per annum to a high of 1200 pesos per year. The highest salaries were paid to those who served in the viceregal capital, Mexico City. The lowest salaries were paid in those customhouses located in the provinces where little or meager economic activity occurred. As operations in the customhouses burgeoned in the late eighteenth century, many of these buildings became so small that they could only sustain operations at a reduced level. A case in point is the customhouse at Veracruz. In 1784, a cry came from aduana officials in Veracruz that the customhouse was no longer large enough to sustain the expanded operations in it as a consequence of the revival of seaborne trade. Ultimately the Royal Corps of Engineers were conscripted to build either a new customhouse or modify the one in service.[16]

Other branches of the Royal Exchequer also cost the viceroyalty a great sum of money to maintain them. When we speak of finances or operational funds we are really talking about outlays to pay for salaries and wages. This further erudition supports the original hypothesis concerning the growth of the patrimonial state and the increased role of the bureaucracy in the Mexican economy. Another illustration is the blackpowder or gunpowder monopoly. This monopoly was created in the aftermath of the Gálvez Visitation of 1765-1771. The headquarters of the bureaucracy was Mexico City; the seat of the viceregal government. The chief gunpowder factory was located in Chapultepec. Blackpowder, by the late colonial period, was used principally in the mines of New Spain, particularly those in Zacatecas and Guanajuato. Expenditures for the administration of the monopoly were quite low in comparison to the income generated.[17] In 1802 Alexander von Humboldt visited the factory of Chapultepec and eventually was allowed to review the financial records of the gunpowder monopoly. He found that in 1802 the total production was valued at 750 thousand pesos. Of this total value, more than 500 thousand pesos were paid to the employees; who produced the blackpowder needed in the mines of the Mexican colony. The net profit to the viceroyalty and its government was the sum of approximately 145 thousand pesos.[18] Table 9 thus illustrates how small were the expenditures and the relatively number of officials necessary for the administration of the monopoly. In terms of the first three positions

TABLE 9 PERSONNEL EXPENDITURES FOR THE GUNPOWDER MONOPOLY, 1790

Official Title	Number	Salary/Pesos
Director	1	4,000
Assayer	1	500
Accountant	1	200
Scribes	3	140
Comptroller	1	130
Guards	3	190
TOTAL	10	5,160

SOURCE: MN, Reyno de México III, ms. 335.

listed in table 9, all were either peninsular or creole. Of course, the Director was a Spaniard as was the assayer. Information could not be located for this study to indicate the ethnicity of the accountant, however, given the prevailing social structure in New Spain, he probably was a creole.[19]

Another branch of the bureaucracy which cost the viceregal government was that of the playing-card (naipes) monopoly. It is yet another monopoly which was established in Bourbon Mexico after Gálvez's Visitation. As table 10 shows, only 16 officials directed the administrative operations of the naipe monopoly.[20] In 1804 Humboldt observed that the income from the sale of naipes totalled 120 thousand pesos. By the early nineteenth century, the colonial bureaucracy, which collected the revenue from playing-card sales, included blackpoweder, snow, pulque, and cockfighting under its jurisdiction.[21] As with the

TABLE 10 PERSONNEL COSTS FOR THE PLAYING-CARD MONOPOLY,1790

Official Title	Number of Men	Salary/Pesos
Director	1	600
Accountant	1	550
Scribe	1	300
Second Class Official	1	125
Third Class Official	1	125
Comptroller	1	125
Cashier	2	174
Accountant (Currency)	2	172
Commandant (Security)	1	200
Lieutenant	1	150
Chief Guard	1	62
Corporals	3	187
TOTAL	16	2,750

SOURCE: MN, Reyno de México III, ms. 335.

other branches examined in this chapter, the playing-card monopoly showed a definite peninsular bias. All of the top officials were Spaniards and very few creoles served in it. Again we conclude that the patrimonial state had grown considerably during the late colonial era and especially during the 1790s.[22]

The intendant reforms of 1786 had a decided impact upon Bourbon Mexico. These ordinances reorganized the colony both politically and economically. Henceforth the structure of the Mexican economy was much more centralized than it had been previously. In particular, the administration of the economy was charged to the intendants and their subordinates.[23] Paramount among the agencies now under the direction of the intendants was that of the Royal Exchequer.

Most of the officials associated with the Royal Exchequer were quartered in Mexico City, although the crown did dispatch exchequer officials to each provincial capital. Quite naturally it was the exchequer officials in Mexico City who had the greatest powers and thus the most prestige.

TABLE 11 PERSONNEL AND EXPENDITURES OF THE ROYAL EXCHEQUER IN MEXICO CITY, 1792

Title/Office	Number of Men	Salaries/Pesos
Chief Accountants	3	13,800
Fiscal Accountants	6	15,000
Second Class Accountants	3	6,600
First Class Regulator	6	10,800
Second Class Regulator	3	4,500
Archivist (Recordkeeper)	1	1,000
Bookeeper	2	1,200
First Class Commentator	6	3,600
Second Class Commentator	6	3,000
Scribe	1	1,000
Porter	1	400
TOTAL	38	59,000

SOURCE: BL, Mexican Manuscripts, vol. 9 and MN, Reyno de México III, ms. 335.

This branch of the colonial government was charged specifically with the collection and dispersal of finances to meet the obligations of the Royal Government located in Mexico City. Its role increased after 1786 and especially during the viceregency of the Second Conde de Revillagigedo. As table 11 shows, the office of the Royal Exchequer in Mexico City had thirty-eight officers in 1792 charged with overseeing the finances of the viceroyalty. The viceroy served both as superintendent and intendant for the Intendancy of Mexico. In comparison to the expenditures, the income of the Royal Exchequer was much greater.[24] Revillagigedo reported in his 1794 Instrucción reservada that the expenditures borne in the administration of Bourbon Mexico amounted to a mere 4.8 million pesos. This figure represents the entire cost of all of the branches of the viceregal government and not just the cost of the Royal Exchequer. According to the documents in the Museo Naval, located in Madrid, Spain, the revenue or income of New Spain totalled nearly 19 million pesos in 1790.[25] If these sums are accurate then we may presume that the Mexican colony had a surplus over expenditures of some 14 million pesos in 1790. And indeed the chronicle of Alexander von Humboldt verifies these estimates. These foregoing estimates illustrate that in the late colonial period, the colonial bureaucracy, for the most part, cost the viceregal government very little in comparison to the revenue they generated.

Yet some branches of the colonial government did indeed cost a great deal in view of their size and their operations in the late Mexican colony. A case in point is the Royal Mint (Casa de Moneda) located in Mexico City. This office, which was connected to the Royal Exchequer, employed some 90 administrators and salaried people as of 1790. In addition, the Royal Mint employed between 450 and 500 men to produce the coinage of this New World realm. In 1790 the viceregal government paid out between 350 and

400 thousand pesos in wages and salaries. This averages out to between 600 and 700 pesos for each person working in the Casa de Moneda. Such sums are quite large considering the prevailing wage rate in late colonial Mexico. True, the chief administrators were paid rather handsomely in contrast to the common laborers in the Royal Mint. However, discounting this fact the sums allocated were quite large in comparison to the numbers employed by the Royal Mint.[26] Still we must also recognize that the costs of fabrication were high in the Royal Mint because of the cost of machinery and other materials. The operation of the mint therefore was not as lucrative, especially for the workers, as one might believe at first glance.

Like the other branches of the colonial bureaucracy, the officials of the Royal Mint reflect the prevailing peninsularization of late colonial Mexico. The Director of the Mint, Don Francisco de Córdoba, was a Spaniard from the province of Malaga. He had served in the mints in Spain prior to his assignment to Bourbon Mexico. As of 1791 about eighty percent of all of the officials were Spaniards in terms of their social origins. Information could not be located to determine the economic strata of the officers serving in the Royal Mint. Most likely the senior officials, such as Córdoba, belonged to the higher economic and social strata of the colony.[27] The remainder of the employees or rather those who actually toiled in the Royal Mint were for the most part either creoles or mestizos. Some Indians also were employed to do some of the common labor involved in the minting process.

By the end of the eighteenth century, most of the prestige posts in the Indies were held by Spaniards. When Don José de Gálvez became the Minister of the Indies in 1776, he initiated a prolonged program to wrest political control from the entrenched creole class in late Bourbon Mexico. The Bourbon reformers had a new vision of the role of New Spain within their imperial scheme. Charles III and his advisers had the notion that the Mexican colony was a patrimony of the crown. The intendant ordinances were enacted in 1786 with this idea in mind. Gálvez and the Conde de Floridablanca agreed that centralization was the keystone of administrative reform in the New World and particularly in Bourbon Mexico. During his now famous visit to the Mexican colony, between 1765 and 1771, Gálvez gained an extensive knowledge concerning the government of New Spain. His clashes with local officials during his residence in Mexico forever made him skeptical of "rule by colonials." When he arrived in Bourbon Mexico he found a society riddled with graft and corruption which he ascribed to the weak Spanish government.[28] The creation and promotion of the patrimonial state therefore became a prime objective of the Bourbon reformers. Spaniards were sent to professionalize the colonial service, and as a means to end the maladministration prevalent in late Bourbon Mexico.

Finances are a requisite to the existence and maintenance of any empire and this is especially accurate with regard to the Spanish empire. As the economy of New Spain grew in the late colonial period so did the revenues generated from taxes. Fiscal reform thereby was a focus of the Bourbon monarchs and late colonial viceroys. Monopolies were created to bring more income into the king's coffers. However, more importantly the fiscal bureaucracies were enlarged considerably after the promulgation of the intendant ordinances and establishment of *comercio libre*. Customhouses were built in all of the major commercial centers in late Bourbon Mexico. The *Real aduana* grew enormously in the late colonial period so that by the early 1790s some 500 customs officers served the viceroyalty; collecting duties on goods sold in New Spain and those products sent abroad.[29] The Royal Exchequer grew both in size and status. In essence, these Spanish officials became a vanguard which transformed the Mexican economy into a patrimonial economy.

By the end of the colonial epoch, the administration of the Mexican economy was almost totally in the hands of Spaniards. The viceroys and other colonial officials changed policies as they deemed necessary and with the concurrence of the crown. For instance, the Conde de Revillagigedo, in 1793 and 1794, wrote the crown informing them of his accomplishments in the field of economic affairs. While in office, he introduced the now famous comercio libre decree, authorized patents for machinery, increased the size of the fiscal bureaucracies, and reformed the marketplaces found throughout Mexico.[30] By far the most important reform was that of the intendants. They were designed as catalysts of both political and economic change. Centralization resulted in more power for Spanish colonial officials, particularly in economic affairs. The intendant ordinances called upon the intendants to promote economic development. Bourbon reformers, such as Gálvez and Revillagigedo, clearly believed that economic progress rested in the hands of capable administrators rather than in the hands of merchants and colonists. Fiscal reform was a double-edged sword. It provided more income to the crown and at the same time centralized economic affairs.

The peninsularization of the colonial service achieved some of the goals of the Bourbon reformers. Foremost, it did succeed in centralizing the colonial government under Spaniards. Decisions concerning the Mexican colony were now controlled by the viceroy and intendants. It did not, however, end the corruption prevalent in New Spain. Although the Spaniards were generally less inclined toward corruption, many did engage in illegal activities. Still, the peninsularization of the colonial government brought profound change to the Mexican colony. The Spaniards serving in Bourbon Mexico were interested in achieving crown objectives, but more importantly, they knew rewards awaited them if they were successful in implementing the king's policies. In essence, the peninsularization of late colonial Mexico meant a greatly expanded patrimonial state and likewise the Mexican economy became increasingly patrimonial in composition and operation. By independence the Bourbon monarchy had reached the zenith of its power and prestige. Patrimonial power, however, also became a reason why the Mexicans ultimately revolted. By 1800 the Mexican elites found themselves effectively shut off from the colonial government and therefore unable to have a voice in the decsions made on their behalf. The patrimonial state nonetheless has remained an enduring legacy in the course of Mexican history.

CHAPTER VIII

THE CONDE DE REVILLAGIGEDO: PROPONENT OF ECONOMIC REFORM?

Historians of late colonial Mexico are well aware of the role of the Second Conde de Revillagigedo in Mexican history. His viceregency, which spanned between 1789 and 1794, is often referred to as a period of "enlightened" rule. He is noted for introducing to late Bourbon Mexico a whole series of reforms which helped to spur economic activity. Unlike his immediate predecessors, the Conde de Revillagigedo believed in an activist role for the viceroy, particularly in economic and political affairs. Revillagigedo utilized the intendants as the conduit of his reforms. Throughout his viceregency he called upon the intendants to keep him abreast of trends in the provinces.[1] Indeed, the Conde de Revillagigedo was both a proponent and catalyst of economic reform. More importantly, however, he was an ardent advocate and supporter of the patrimonial state existing in the late Mexican colony. Revillagigedo was clearly sent to New Spain by the Bourbon king, Charles IV, to increase regalist authority and to assert direct control over the Mexican economy.

The future Conde de Revillagigedo and viceroy of New Spain was born in Cuba to an aristocratic Spanish family. He would become in the late eighteenth century the patriarch of this wealthy and prestigious family. While still a small boy, his father, the First Conde de Revillagigedo, was named the viceroy of the Mexican colony. The first Conde de Revillagigedo served as viceroy between 1746 and 1755. Although his viceregency was rather uneventful by eighteenth century standards, this experience had an important impact on his son; the future Second Conde de Revillagigedo. Young Revillagigedo enjoyed his residence in the Mexican colony. He was intrigued by both its expanse and diversity. At this time, however, he showed little evidence of desiring a career in the king's service. Yet this is what did transpire after the second Conde de Revillagigedo reached maturity. Before he could enter royal service his father decided that he needed a good education. The first Conde de Revillagigedo consequently sent his son back to Spain to prepare for his future career. He obtained a rather extensive education and more importantly was exposed to the concepts of the French Enlightenment. He showed particular interest in the study of economics or political economy as it was so named in the eighteenth century.[2] These studies, which included military science, later assisted him in the administration of the viceroyalty of New Spain. His economic studies undoubtedly influenced the economic policies and reforms which he instituted in the late colonial period.

Revillagigedo arrived in Bourbon Mexico in 1789 after a seaward voyage from Spain and quickly made his way to the viceregal capital, Mexico City. He took up residence in the viceregal palace and convened both the intendants and heads of the various government branches. He informed them that he had been sent to Mexico serve his and their monarch, Charles IV. From the outset Revillagigedo took a belligerent stance toward the *audiencia* and its officials. He had a general contempt, as noted previously, for the creole elite whom he believed had far too much power and influence within the viceregal court. As well as being viceroy of New Spain, the Conde de Revillagigedo was the intendant for the Province of Mexico and superintendent of the Royal Exchequer.[3] Revillagigedo is noted for the many reforms which he enacted during the course of his viceregency. Far less, however, is known about his career as a promoter and advocate of economic reform. Was the Conde de Revillagigedo actually an economic reformer? What kinds of actions and proposals did he make during his viceregency?

In 1790 the Conde de Revillagigedo reported to officials in Madrid concerning the implementation of the intendant ordinances. The viceroy saw the intendants primarily as economic agents for the crown. He observed that the intendants and reformed <u>aduanas</u> had successfully expanded the income for this New World colony. Documents found both in Spain and Mexico verify Revillagigedo's observations and comments.[4] By 1794 the viceroyalty of New Spain had an income of some 50 million pesos from all sources and expenditures which totalled 38 million pesos, thereby leaving the Mexican colony with a surplus of nearly 12 million pesos. The Royal Exchequer alone had an income of 19 million pesos and expenses of 13 million pesos. The surplus produced during the late colonial period was nonetheless impressive considering the operations borne by the viceregal government. Additional treasuries and <u>aduanas</u> had to be constructed to house the ever increasing funds flowing into the viceregal coffers. New Spain, like the European continent, was undergoing an economic boom; caused in part by the revival of mining and the rise of the capitalist-mercantilist world economy. Revillagigedo, for his part, believed that the economic boom resulted from the increased role of the colonial bureaucracy in directing and reforming economic affairs.[5]

Revillagigedo was a rather prolific writer and took his position as viceroy very seriously. From the outset of his administration he began to amass a large amount of records to attest to the economic development taking place in the Mexican colony during his viceregency. In 1793, using these collected records, he wrote a massive report about the strengths and weaknesses of Mexico's political economy. This report was basically a summarization of the steps taken in the period between 1789 and 1793 to foster economic growth. Chief among his observations was that both mining and agriculture showed great advances during his viceregency. Revillagigedo calculated that agriculture had grown three fold during the 1780s. He derived these estimates from the tithe collections which came from the papers and records housed in the viceregal palace.[6] Later Alexander von Humboldt cited these same figures to indicate how agriculture had development during the late colonial era.

It is evident in Revillagigedo's writings that he considered the revitalization of commerce in Bourbon Mexico as a keystone of the ongoing economic reform program. From the outset he was an ardent supporter of the crown's _comercio libre_ (free trade) policy. As we have already witnessed, _comercio libre_ was not free trade in the parleance of the presentday. It was a system which denied foreign participation or access and encouraged trade between Spain and her colonial possessions in the New World. Noting in 1793 the success of _comercio libre_, Revillagigedo reported to Diego Gardoquí that both Spain and Spanish Mexico had benefited from this "enlightened" policy.[7] At the time of Revillagigedo's viceregency, New Spain exported nearly 33 million pesos worth of goods to Europe, particularly to the Spanish peninsula. Imports into the viceroyalty by contrast totalled nearly 20 million pesos in 1794. By 1802 Mexico's trade through Veracruz had grown to just over 60 million pesos.[8] Revillagigedo considered these figures as both a vindication and testament to the success achieved under <u>comercio libre</u>. Indeed, the viceroy had much praise for the "free trade" policy instituted by the Spanish Bourbons. But Revillagigedo was starkly aware that continued commercial reform was necessary if <u>comercio libre</u> was to remain a fruitful policy.

In 1794 Revillagigedo reported that contraband continued to be a plague which drained both royal and viceregal coffers of untold wealth. Contraband trade thrived in the New World from the sixteenth to eighteenth centuries as a consequence of Spain's restrictive commercial system. With the implementation of <u>comercio libre</u>, Viceroy Revillagigedo could no longer find a rational reason for the existence of the contraband trade. Between 1790 and 1794 he sent repeated letters to Spanish officials in Madrid about the steps he had undertaken to curtail clandestine smuggling activities. In 1792 he authorized an outlay of 100 thousand pesos to strengthen the <u>guarda costas</u>. He even called upon the

Havana fleet to intercept smugglers. The Conde de Revillagigedo believed that contrabandists should be considered privateers and as such should be treated as criminals once apprehended. To this end he decided to impose harsher penalties on smugglers. Henceforth a contrabandist on the first offense would receive 100 lashes. If he were caught a second time he would have his right hand severed. If this did not succeed in dissuading, upon the third offense, he would be hung.[9] A number of people died in this manner during the late colonial and independence era.

It is evident that the commerce of New Spain grew markedly during the viceregency of the Conde de Revillagigedo. While he ascribed this boom of the Mexican economy to comercio libre, we are forced to look at the total world view of the late eighteenth century. Europe underwent an economic revolution at the mid-point of the eighteenth century. Great Britain, for instance, saw a thriving sugar and textile industry during this identical period. Economic historians disagree upon the complete reasons for the sudden spurt in the world economy. There are, however, several explanations for this expansion during the late eighteenth century. By the 1750s the European continent had an emerging middle or mercantile class who had excess capital to invest. This is manifested in the growth of the merchant classes both in Europe and the New World. Science had also improved by the mid-eighteenth century and thereby longevity had increased even among the lower social strata. This enlarged population demanded an increased supply of goods and merchants, in search of ever increasing wealth, provided these goods.[10] More importantly, the structure of government had also changed. Instead of discouraging economic initiative government now promoted it. In essence, Spain promoted a patrimonial state which encouraged economic development. In the case of Spanish America and in particular Mexico the transformation of government spurred on the development of the patrimonial economy.

New Spain, like Spain and Europe, underwent a great deal of change in the eighteenth century. As the population rebounded from the declines of the sixteenth and seventeenth centuries so flowed the Mexican economy. By the mid-point of the eighteenth century, the mining industry of Bourbon Mexico showed remarkable activity and growth. By 1800 the population had risen to over five million souls. As a consequence, demand for both luxuries and necessities increased greatly. Merchants throughout the country rushed to fill this demand and thereby enrich themselves. Transatlantic commerce between Spain and Mexico rebounded as well. Government revenues rose and thus the viceregal government embarked on a massive public works program. Merchants and hacendados diversified their investments to both expand and protect their wealth. The enactment of the intendant ordinances in 1786 became the first salvo in resurrecting and protecting the patrimonial state. Revillagigedo is the very embodiment of the Age of Reason in the New World. He promoted the interests of the Bourbon monarchy, which included the promotion of economic development and centralized government. He was an ardent supporter of the intendant and economic reforms which curbed the political and economic influence of the colonial elites of New Spain.[11] His successors, the Marqués de Branciforte and Miguel José de Azanza, were also advocates of the patrimonial state although they adopted different policies.

From the outset of his viceregency the second Conde de Revillagigedo believed in an activist state, particularly in dealing with economic affairs. An example is his use of the colonial bureaucracy in promoting the expansion of the Mexican economy. As we have noted previously, the level of commercial activity in late colonial Mexico forced the viceregal government to respond by establishing more customhouses and increasing the size of the _Real aduana_. Under the tutelage of Don Miguel Paez the _Real aduana_ grew in importance and became a keystone in the finances of the Mexican colony. Paez, very early on, gained the confidence and friendship of the Conde de Revillagigedo. The viceroy responded to the superintendent's request for additional personnel and in 1790 also authorized additional funding for the Real aduana.[12] Revillagigedo consequently enlisted the support of the Royal Corps of Engineers to construct and repair the customhouses found throughout New Spain. In 1794 construction began on the customhouses in Tlaxcala and Zacatecas. The customhouse in Veracruz also was given a facelift and repaired.[13] Between 1789 and 1794 the size of the Real aduana grew from some 300 men to well over 400 men. An increase in state revenues accompanied the enlargement of the Real aduana.[14] Revillagigedo saw his role in economic affairs as a promoter of the patrimonial state and an ever increasing financial base in the Mexican colony. Revenues were essential to the viceregal government's ability to sustain its operations.

Revillagigedo's Instrucción reservada to the Marqués de Branciforte clearly illustrates his knowledge of economic theory. Throughout his viceregency he advocated the development of infrastructure. Chief among his concerns was that of improving Bourbon Mexico's communication links. Revillagigedo was a proponent of building roads from Mexico City to Veracruz and Acapulco because they were the chief entrepôts of trade. Upon assuming the office of viceroy, he carefully reviewed the reports on roadbuilding left by his predecessors. One report in particular caught his eye and made him resolute in his commitment to improve Mexico's highways. In 1768 Ricardo Alymer was given the task of designing a road from the viceregal capital, Mexico City, to Toluca.[15] Alymer subsequently finished the designs and sent them to viceregal authorities. These plans, however, were not acted upon until the beginning of the Revillagigedo viceregency. The viceroy placed the entire project in the capable hands of <u>corregidor</u> Don Bernardo Bonavía in 1791. Funding, from the outset, appeared to be the major obstacle to the completion of this project. Revillagigedo eventually decided to extract road tolls from travellers and merchants to help defray the costs of the project. Bonavía subsequently contacted Don Miguel del Corral, Director of the Royal Corps of Engineers in New Spain, and asked for assistance on the project. Engineer Manuel Mascaró was placed in charge with Don Diego García Conde as his lieutenant. On 25 November 1793 work began on the Toluca road.[16] In the succeeding viceregencies of the Marqués de Branciforte and Miguel José de Azanza, the road was finally completed. The Conde de Revillagigedo also succeeded in promoting roadbuilding elsewhere in New Spain such as the roads built to seaports of Acapulco and Veracruz.[17] It is clear that he considered roadbuilding an essential step in commercial development in the Mexican colony. But the the viceroy also was an advocate of better roads to increase the powers of the patrimonial state.

Another example of his efforts involving public works in New Spain was the Real desagüe located around Mexico City. This massive system of drainage canals were built for the most part during the seventeenth century to relieve the capital from the floods which plagued it from 1550 onwards.[18] By the early 1790s the viceregal capital had grown considerably since the seventeenth century. In fact, Mexico City by the late eighteenth century was the most populous city in the Western Hemisphere. Consequently, the city had outgrown its boundaries. The barrios of Mexico City underwent flooding during the late 1770s and 1780s. Such an occurrence necessitated some kind of remedy from the viceregal government. When the second Conde de Revillagigedo entered the capital in 1789 he found reports indicating that his predecessors had engaged the services of Engineer Ricardo Alymer in solving the flooding problem.[19] Viceroy Revillagigedo wholeheartedly endorsed Alymer's proposals. Alymer had proposed an extension of the canals and more importantly the dredging of the principal canals surrounding Mexico City. In addition, Alymer recommended that the desagüe's lining be repaired with a new base of lime. Funding, however, clouded the project during much of 1789.

Merchants of the Mexico City Consulado caught wind of the financial problems of the desagüe and in early 1790 gave nearly 100 thousand pesos to the viceregal government.

Revillagigedo was grateful but suspicious of this generosity. In July 1790 he sent a letter to the Prior of the Consulado, Don José de Cevallos, thanking the merchant organization for their assistance and cooperation in the desague project.[20] The motivation of the merchants' contribution to the desagüe is uncertain although most likely they expected to gain financially and economically from its execution. The probable rationale was that the end of flooding would create a healthy commercial climate. Their shops and wares most likely would not be flooded henceforth, thereby reducing the costs borne in commercial activities. Indeed after 1790 the flooding problem all but disappeared leaving Mexico City merchants free to pursue their commercial activities.[21]

As superintendent of the Royal Exchequer, the Conde de Revillagigedo took his role very seriously and executed this office with much vigor. To improve the status and functioning of the Royal Exchequer he authorized the expenditure of 98,316 pesos in 1791-1793 to undertake a facelift of all of the Cajas reales located in the major urban centers of the Mexican colony. The Royal Corps of Engineers were again used in these operations. The repairs and facelift made on the Caja real in Mexico City became the standard blueprint for those in the remainder of New Spain.[22] Viceroy Revillagigedo apparently believed that these renovations would enhance exchequer operations.

It is, however, hard to believe that this step alone promoted economic development in the viceroyalty. For each year of the Revillagigedo viceregency revenues generated by the Royal Exchequer did rise. Moreover, the Conde de Revillagigedo undoubtedly assisted in the economic expansion of the late colonial period.[23] His importance nonetheless rests largely with his promotion of the patrimonial state and thereby support for a patrimonial economy.

Revillagigedo arrived in Bourbon Mexico with a prescribed notion of government. He believed in a strong centralized state which was charged with reforming conditions found in the New World. He had been taught that the Enlightenment should be incorporated into every facet of Mexican society. To this end he was willing to do battle with any interest or class which was in conflict with the basic tenets of the Caroline reforms. In 1793 he wrote a detailed report concerning the achievements of the Caroline economic reforms.[24] Revillagigedo, as noted earlier, was an ardent supporter of comercio libre and throughout his report he extolled the virtues of this policy as it affected the late Mexican colony. The viceroy, however, saw many obstacles to the continued economic progress in New Spain. In particular, he criticized the colonial bureaucracy and especially the Council of the Indies for not granting the intendants and viceroy greater powers in economic affairs. Politics therefore formed the basis for his attacks on the colonial elites.

Viceroy Revillagigedo first attacked local government. He observed that their control of the Mexican populace hindered economic development. The *cabildos* and *ayuntamientos*, he noted, served only their interests and that of the crown. He claimed that these bodies were the bastion of graft and corruption in the Mexican colony. Revillagigedo reported that these political entities seldom met and thus their members collected a salary with little or no toil at all. When they did meet, they rarely acted in the crown's favor but rather in accordance with the desires of the vested colonial elites. Next, Viceroy Revillagigedo criticized the power of the *Consulado* of Mexico City. Throughout his viceregency he observed that the merchants had raised their prices even though their costs had actually decreased in the aftermath of the extension of *comercio libre* in 1789. This corporate body, he concluded, was detrimental to the crown's and colonial government's plans for promoting economic development. He consequently believed that they constituted a monopoly which should be overturned or severely curtailed.[25] To end the predominance of the Mexico City *Consulado*, he proposed the establishment of additional merchant guilds. His proposal, however, was not acted upon until he left the Mexican scene. His successor, the Marqués de Branciforte, ultimately gained the necessary permission to create two new *consulados* in New Spain. In 1795 the *consulados* of Veracruz and Guadalajara were established over the vehement protestations of the Mexico City merchants.[26]

Another corporate body or entrenched elite which the Conde de Revillagigedo attacked in his 1793 report was that of the artisan guild. Throughout the Mexican colony, especially in the major commercial centers, artisans were organized into monopolistic guilds. As with his observations concerning the Mexico City *Consulado*, he noted that the artisans of New Spain tried to restrain commerce. By withholding guild membership to many individuals they were able to maintain their price levels. More importantly, the Conde de Revillagigedo claimed that they used Indian laborers to produce their wares while excluding them from guild membership. These Indians and mestizos, who toiled for the artisans, were not well trained and were paid substandard wages. Indeed, he had noted upon his entrance into the viceregal capital in 1789 that many of these apprenticed people lived on the streets or in slums as a consequence of the poor wages paid to them. To remedy this situation Revillagigedo proposed that the intendants and viceroys be given authority to issue charters to guilds and "inspect their practices." Like so many of his proposals, the guild proposal apparently fell on largely deaf ears in Madrid.[27]

Revillagigedo did not direct his criticisms entirely on the urban elites or interests. He also turned his tongue onto the landholding elites in late Bourbon Mexico. The viceroy observed that the Catholic Church controlled or owned much of the land in New Spain. The Church owned haciendas; operating them and in many cases renting them out. Revillagigedo claimed that because of their special status the Church paid few taxes. The viceroy criticized this development and concluded that the Church was largely a rentier who risked little and contributed few funds for the administration of the Mexican viceroyalty. To avert this situation the viceroy apparently believed in some form of direct royal control over these Church lands although he did not state it in his 1793 report. Another group engaged in the same activities as the Catholic Church were the private _hacendados_ of New Spain. Revillagigedo believed that this landholding class was detrimental to Mexican economic development as well as the aims of the Bourbon reformers in Spain and the New World. He reasoned that their constant drive to acquire more land, instead of increasing agricultural production, only facilitated their increased wealth and social status. As a social class, the _hacendados_ acted almost like semi-autonomous lords. Revillagigedo noted that the _hacendado_ class constituted a state within a state and a class which sooner or later would have to be confronted.[28] The viceroy's desire to redistribute New Spain's fertile lands emanated primarily from a political desire rather than from an egalitarian motive. Throughout his viceregency the Conde de Revillagigedo supported the growth of the patrimonial state and was opposed to any group or class in conflict with it.

One of the more important areas of the Mexican economy which concerned him was that of mining. From the dawn of Spanish Mexico, in the sixteenth century, mining played a pivotal role. As we noted previously, Zacatecas and Guanajuato were the chief producers of precious metals during the late colonial period. Without silver neither Spain nor Bourbon Mexico could long persevere. One of the chief methods used by Revillagigedo to promote mining and mining technology was through the Royal College of Mining located in Mexico City. As an ardent supporter of the Enlightenment, the Conde de Revillagigedo also supported what we call today science and technology. Upon assuming his position as viceroy, he called upon the Mining College to produce texts and pamphlets which would assist in the revitalization of the Mexican mining industry. One work on mining prompted by Revillagigedo stands out in the late colonial era. In 1792 José Antonio Ribera Sánchez published a treatise on mining methods utilized throughout New Spain. Sánchez's book is principally a historical-analytical study of mining production in Spanish Mexico from the seventeenth century up to 1790. It contains interesting details on the so-called patio process and his diagrams explain various production techniques.[29] Whether the Sánchez treatise was ever widely used is doubtful, however, it evidences Revillagigedo's concern for economic progress in the late Mexican colony.

Throughout his viceregency the Conde de Revillagigedo strove to promote economic development. To this end, in 1792-1793, he sent out the intendants of New Spain to collect as much economic data as possible from the provinces. These reports were later used to make decisions in the administration of the economy.[30] The Conde de Revillagigedo is also noted for the creation of the Archivo General de México which later was transformed into the Archivo General de la Nación. At the end of his viceregency he made several proposals for the production of *lino* and *cañamo*. A more detailed explanation of this nascent industry can be found in Chapter 2 of this present study. The viceroy was an articulate advocate of his ideas concerning economic development and most of his records are still preserved in Spanish and Mexican archives. In fact, for colonial Mexican historians his viceregal records are probably the most complete for any viceroy or official who served in the late colonial period.

From the outset of his viceregency, the Conde de Revillagigedo was an advocate of the centralization policies undertaken by the Bourbon monarchy.[31] He was a keen observer of colonial society and understood the dynamics of power in that setting. More importantly, for the present study, he was a proponent of the patrimonial state. The intendants as well as the viceroy were utilized to fulfill the goals of the Bourbon monarchs. The Conde de Revillagigedo clashed with the Mexico City merchants and artisans on the basis of regalism. He believed that crown power should be aobsolute both in political and economic affairs. Centralization became the cornerstone of Bourbon economic reform. The colonial bureaucracy increased its power and thereby helped to foster a state-crafted economy. Patrimonialism became a major tenet of Caroline economic reforms and Revillagigedo was one of its most ardent supporters. Henceforth bureaucrats were used to both control and promote economic development in New Spain.

Revillagigedo offered a great many reforms to New Spain between 1789 and 1794. He enlisted the services of the Royal Corps of Engineers to improve the infrastructure of Bourbon Mexico. He encouraged the development of technology, particularly in the field of mining. The viceroy supported comercio libre and subsequently drafted a set of codes for Mexico's marketplaces. To protect the merchants who carried their wares across the breadth of Mexico he appropriated funds for road construction and ultimately strengthened the police force which patrolled these roads.[32]

Revillagigedo fought the entrenched economic interests of the colony, most notably the Church, *hacendados*, and merchants, to assert monarchical and viceregal authority. He was clearly a child of the Enlightenment and consequently fashioned his economic thoughts on its tenets. The viceroy believed the state should be paramount in economic affairs and not to local capitalist interests who were primarily interested in fostering their wealth. Revillagigedo concluded in 1794 that the colonial elites were a hindrance to Mexican economic development. While the viceroy was decidedly in favor of economic progress his actions were skewed in favor of the patrimonial state. Nonetheless, by the beginning of the nineteenth century, Mexico was the most prosperous of Spain's possessions in the New World.[33] Ahead lay a half-century of civil wars and economic chaos.

CHAPTER IX

ECONOMIC THOUGHT, REVOLUTION, AND INDEPENDENCE

In the aftermath of the viceregency of the Conde de Revillagigedo the situation in Bourbon Mexico soon deteriorated. The outbreak of the French Revolution and the subsequent excesses of the Reign of Terror profoundly affected the Bourbon monarchy in Spain. Charles IV was shocked by the execution of Louis XVI and considered the French Republic a contagion which might spread to his own realm if left unchecked. The Spanish king therefore allied himself with the European powers to rid themselves of the French Republic. Such an undertaking forced Charles IV to spend heavily for warfare and even to borrow large sums of money. At the end of Revillagigedo's viceregency, New Spain was the chief source of surplus funds. Colonial bureaucrats collected nearly fifty million pesos and spent little more than thirty-eight million pesos, thus leaving New Spain a twelve million peso surplus which was transported to the king's coffers in Madrid.[1] Taxes rose and the colonial elites were forced to contribute to Spain's continental campaigns. The colonial bureaucrats continued to assert their dominance and the colonial elites found themselves virtually without representation in the colonial government. Bureaucrats believed that any outburst by the elites as an attack on the patrimonial state--an act tantamount to treason. Few bureaucrats nor viceroys considered the Mexican elites as an economic class or an economic minded group. Both assumptions and the centralized government of the late colonial period helped to foster tension and discontent within the Mexican colony. While the colonial elites could accept political deprivation in favor of the king's officials, they could not tolerate the Mexican economy being entirely dominated by Spain. The development of economic thought and the increased wealth of the colonial merchants led to an evitable clash between them and the colonial bureaucracy. In essence, the imprisonment of Ferdinand VII became a pretext and prelude to Mexican Independence.[2]

Economic thought changed in both Spain and Mexico during the course of the eighteenth century. In Spain, the entrance of the Bourbons, at the beginning of the eighteenth century, gave birth to an intellectual renaissance, particularly in the field of political economy. This renaissance was spurred on by the ideas of the French Enlightenment. Of main concern to the new Spanish monarch, Phillip V, was the renovation of the

Spanish economy. His tutor and mentor, Louis XIV, encouraged him to promote the study of political economy in Spanish universities. French economist consequently sent their treatises to Spain for their use in universities. Soon Spanish intellectuals began to assert themselves and produced their own works which called for economic reform in Spain as well as the Indies.[3] In 1724 Jerónimo de Uztaríz wrote a work which criticized the Hapsburg system of taxation which retarded economic growth. He urged the Bourbon monarchy to abandon this system and replace it with a drastically lowered tax system to encourage seaborne commerce. The Spanish economist also called upon the monarchy to promote and encourage entrepreneurship, particularly with regard to Spanish textile merchants and manufacturers.[4] Uztaríz's words struck a responsive cord and within the next decade most of his proposals were enacted by the Bourbon reformers in Madrid.

The success of the Uztaríz proposals spurred on further economy inquiry. Bernardo de Ulloa in 1734 published a treatise which raised some of the same questions posed by Uztaríz. Ulloa found the decline of Spanish commerce deplorable, which he attributed to the inept Hapsburg monarchy. Ulloa also considered the British and French Antilles as a threat to Spain's hegemony in the New World.[5] Unlike Uztaríz most of

Ulloa's proposals were not acted upon by officials in Madrid. The Spain of Ulloa, however, was not capable of meeting the British challenge in the Caribbean because of her small navy. The wars of the 1740s with the British nonetheless resulted in a massive naval development program. With the reign of Charles III (1759-1788), the Spanish navy gained back much of its supremacy and even assisted in the Americans gaining their independence from Great Britain during the 1770s.[6]

The most important work of the eighteenth century was clearly that of José Campillo y Cossío who served as a minister to Phillip V. As a member of the Spanish government during the early stages of the eighteenth century, he was privy to most sensitive information concerning the Spanish economy. His treatise, which was finally published in 1789, forever changed the course of Spanish and Mexican history. Quite remarkably, Campillo called for the complete renovation of colonial administration. The minister also advocated other economic and political reforms. Chief among his proposals which were eventually enacted by the Bourbon reformers was that of <u>comercio libre</u> and the intendants.[7] During the mid-eighteenth century another Spanish economist resurrected Campillo's ideas. Bernardo Ward, although of Irish ancestry, was able to convince Charles III of the validity of Campillo's assertions concerning political and economic reform.[8]

Beginning in 1763, in the aftermath of the Seven Years War, Charles III began a new program to restore Spanish grandeur. Campillo and Ward's views became the cornerstone of the reform program. Charles III and his ministers consequently became convinced of the necessity to centralize administration and economic affairs in the Spanish American colonies. Reforms, such as those borne by the intendants and exchequer officials, were the tools of centralization and the patrimonial state.

By the time of Charles III's death in 1788, the Spanish monarchy was able to reassert itself, especially in economic and political affairs. The Conde de Aranda, the Marqués de Sonora (José de Gálvez), and the Conde de Floridablanca served the Spanish crown well during the eighteenth century. Charles IV, although less capable than his father, inherited a revitalized nation and empire. Charles III nonetheless gained the title of enlightened despot because of his belief in the patrimonial state and his style of absolutist rule. He embraced the basic tenets of the Enlightenment which centered around the idea that man could achieve great progress through personal initiative. Even British economists were affected by the Physiocrats. In 1776 Adam Smith published his now famous *The Wealth of Nations*. This work received a lot of attention by Spanish intellectuals who saw virtue in many of Smith's concepts. One who had a great impact on Spanish economic theory and who adopted many of Smith's economic theories was Don Álvaro Flórez Estrada.[9]

Estrada was born in the 1750s and studied at the famous University of Salamanca. Shortly after Adam Smith's book appeared in print Flórez Estrada obtained a copy of it. From the outset he was intrigued by Smith's analysis. He became particularly interested in the concept of complete free trade. Smith was a vocal critic of British and European restraints on commerce. Estrada subsequently received copies of Quesnay's works and at that point decided to write his own monumental work. Finally in 1812 he published his own book which advocated the total abolition of restraints on trade. In his work he noted the great economic achievements which occurred as a consequence of the enactment of *comercio libre* in 1778. Estrada observed that between 1778 and 1800 Spanish commerce with the colonies increased nearly 500 percent. The Spanish economist stated that the reason for this marked increase emanated directly from the policy of *comercio libre*. He therefore proposed that Spain adopt a policy of total free trade on the British model.[10] The Cádiz junta sponsored the publication of Flórez Estrada's book and also agreed with his prescription to revive the Hispanic economy. The absence of a Spanish monarch intensified desires for a complete reformation of the economy, however, with the return of Ferdinand VII in 1815 liberalism became a very unpopular philosophy to hold. Ferdinand restored the absolutist state and imprisoned liberals whom he viewed as radicals and supporters of republicanism. Although Estrada lived into the 1830s he never saw the enactment of total free trade. Still Estrada did have an impact on Spanish and Mexican economic theory. Undoubtedly, Mexican economic theorists such as Vicente Basadre and José María Quirós were affected by Estrada's analysis during the early nineteenth century.

While Mexican intellectuals espoused the general tenets of the Enlightenment during the late eighteenth century, they did accept all of the doctrines advocated by this movement. Indeed, the Mexican scientists and philosophers adopted a strictly New World variety of the Enlightenment. Science, technology, and economic theory were intertwined with the Mexican Enlightenment.[11] José Antonio de Alzate y Ramírez was a key figure of this movement during the late colonial period. He produced many scientific and economic studies during the course of his long life. Two works in particular stand out with regard to the present study. In 1777 Alzate completed his Report about the Nature, Cultivation, and Benefits from Cochineal.[12] Alzate's work is both scientific and economic in composition. In essence, he describes the history, economics, and politics of cochineal production in the Mexican colony. Cochineal was the most important product of the intendancy of Oaxaca and continued to be so until well into the nineteenth century. Alzate called upon less restrictions on its production as well as an increased price to spur its development. The Mexican scientist and political economist was especially critical of the taxation associated with cochineal harvesting.[13] This treatise, although important, received scant attention from colonial officials and intellectuals.

Later, in the early 1780s, Alzate wrote another important treatise in response to the famine experienced in New Spain during that period. Death and malnutrition accompanied the famine. It created both shock and confusion among the officialdom of the late Mexican colony. Alzate was an observer of the misery which food shortages caused and consequently decided that scientific inquiry might resolve the situation. The Mexican savant believed that Mexican agriculture was on a collision course because of the overuse of some lands and the underuse of others. Alzate noted that many land tracts, especially in northern Mexico, could be reclaimed with improved irrigation. Unlike similar reports of the same historical period, Alzate actually experimented with different crops in the Bajío region. He found that with the use of irrigation both wheat and maize production could be substantially increased in the Bajío. Alzate consequently believed that this corollary held true for the remainder of the Mexican colony as well. In his treatise the Mexican intellectual and scientist claimed that crop yields could be spurred with better crop rotation on overextended lands such as those found in central Mexico.[14] Again, Alzate's proposals only received scant attention from the colonial Mexican government. In late colonial Mexico, little heed was paid to unofficial reports, at least until the early nineteenth century.

Notwithstanding this apathy concerning economic thought among the colonial officialdom, many bureaucrats offered reports which became the basis for the transformation of economic thought during the late colonial and independence periods. In the period between 1789 and 1799 it was primarily the colonial bureaucrats and entrepreneurs who developed economic theory in New Spain. A case in point, as we noted previously, was the career or viceregency of the second Conde de Revillagigedo who instituted many economic and political reforms into the late Mexican colony. In 1793 he completed his ninety some page *Report on the State of Trade in New Spain*. This treatise was basically an attack on monopolies and those who coveted them in Bourbon Mexico.[15] It is a rather vehement attack on the government, politics, and economy of New Spain, which he felt was dominated by the creole elite to the detriment of both the colony and the Spanish crown. It must, however, be remembered that

Viceroy Revillagigedo was a strong supporter of the patrimonial state and therefore opposed any group which might be a hindrance to its continued growth. In essence, he believed that the economy of New Spain should support the objectives of the Spanish empire rather than just the interests of the creole elite. Unlike his predecessors, such as Alzate, Revillagigedo succeeded in convincing the crown to enact many of his proposals.[16] His successor, the Marqués de Branciforte, also tried to economic reforms. He was, however, far less successful than the Conde de Revillagigedo. In many cases the Marqués de Branciforte tried to rescind many of the economic and fiscal measures initiated by his predecessor because of his hatred and suspicion of Enlightenment thought.[17]

In 1793 Charles IV embarked on a war with the renegade French Republic. He allied himself with most of the European monarchs again the French contagion. To finance this costly war he was forced to issue <u>vales reales</u> (bonds) and even their issuance did not succeed in turning the tide of the war in favor of the Spaniards. Indeed, the Bourbon monarchy abandoned the war and signed a humiliating peace treaty with the French Republic. Charles IV, early on in the conflict, determined that Spain could no longer afford to prosecute the war. This treaty, however, put Spain into direct conflict with Great Britain. The new war with Great Britain also placed new strain on the weak Spanish economy.

British naval forces effectively cutoff Spain from her overseas empire and thus the Spanish crown had to adopt a policy of limited neutral shipping. In 1805 the Spanish navy was destroyed at Trafalgar and meanwhile Napoleon Bonaparte established his "continental" system, effectively bottling up the Spanish economy. These events devastated the Hispanic economy and caused political tensions which helped to lead to the Napoleonic invasion and Charles IV's abdication in March 1808. Ferdinand VII's reign, however, was curtailed with the French occupation of the Iberian peninsula. Although Joseph Bonaparte was installed as Spain's monarch, Spanish American officials and other elites refused to recognize his authority.[18] Instead, they continued to rule in Ferdinand's name and following Spanish precedent established juntas to rule in the absence of a Bourbon monarch.

Events in Spain during the late eighteenth century had a decided impact on developments in late Bourbon Mexico. Beginning in 1789 and throughout the remainder of the eighteenth century the crown increased the tax burden in the Mexican colony. The social class most affected by the increasing tax burden was that of the creole _hacendados_ and the nobility.[19] Henceforth the colonial elite paid a higher tax to create a _mayorazgo_ (entail). Starting in 1795 a 15 percent tax was enacted against the formation of any _mayorazgo_ and the rate continued to climb until in 1818 it had risen to 25 percent. This action by the Spanish crown both alarmed and frustrated the colonial elites.[20] Spain's continuing conflict in Europe depleted the king's coffers and by 1799 the Spanish government was on the verge of bankruptcy. In that year the crown enacted the Royal Law of Consolidation in Spain. Spain's finances still worsened further and in 1804 the consolidation law was applied to the Mexican setting. Almost overnight the Mexican elites protested this action, however, the program only lasted four years. Although great sums had been extracted from the Mexican viceroyalty, the Napoleonic invasion of Iberia ended the program. Because of the discontent among the Mexican populace over the Consolidation Law Viceroy José de Iturrigaray finally ended it during 1808.[21]

It is not accurate moreover to believe that New Spain was an intellectual backwater during the late colonial period. Mexico had such talented individuals as José Antonio de Alzate y Ramírez, Antonio de León y Gama, and José Ignacio Bartolache. More importantly, by the late eighteenth century, the development of economic theory was beginning to flourish among the merchant elite and their representative, the _consulados_. In 1788 Manuel Antonio Valdés began to publish the _Gaceta de México_ which carried official news and even economic information. It was the merchants who pr-vided the articles and essays on the Mexican economy. Nearly every facet of the economy was examined in each issue of the Gaceta.[22] Beginning in the early nineteenth century, the successor to the Gaceta, the Diario de México, also adopted a similar format. The publisher of the Diario, Don José de Zuniga y Ontiveros, encouraged the Mexico City, Veracruz, and Guadalajara consulados to submit pieces on the Mexican economy for publication. Two merchants stand out for their literary contributions about the Mexican economy. Both Vicente Basadre and José María Quiros wrote essays during the early nineteenth century which challenged the economic policies followed by the Spanish monarchy. As members of the prestigious Consulado of Veracruz they had a great deal to lose from the deterioration of transatlantic commerce.[23]

During July 1807 Vicente Basadre, ex-secretary of the Veracruz consulado, wrote an intriguing essay to Manuel Godoy concerning Spain's overseas trade and the effects of comercio libre. A cornerstone of Basadre's analysis was that Spanish hegemony and economic prosperity rested on the development of seaborne commerce. The merchant consequently attacked the crown for its restraints on "free trade." Basadre observed that contraband trade was encouraged by the actions of the Spanish government of Charles IV. To resolve the contraband problem the merchant called upon the crown to relax all trade restrictions. During the interlude which accompanied the Peace of Amiens (1802), all Spanish American ports were opened up to trade and Veracruz was a primary beneficiary of this liberalized trade policy. Basadre also noted that in order to make his proposal work it was necessary to expand the Spanish textile industry. He went on further to claim that the British textile industry could not remain predominant if his policies were adopted. Basadre believed it was also important to spur the education of merchants through the establishment of crown sponsored academies. He observed that it was paramount to improve the status of the mercantile professions. Basadre was especially critical of the Mexico City merchants whom he considered were essentially monopolists. He therefore called upon the Spanish crown to restrain "this wealthy rabble."[24] Because of the Napoleonic invasion in 1808 officials in Madrid apparently did not have enough time to act on Basadre's proposals.

Another Mexican economist from the Veracruz _consulado_ who influenced the development of economic theory was Don José María Quirós. He was the secretary of the Veracruz merchants' guild during the early nineteenth century and as such helped direct its administration. From the outset of his service he was an ardent supporter of the policy of _comercio libre_. In 1817 he wrote two important treatises concerning the state or condition of the Mexican economy. The first, Reflections on the Free Trade of the Americas, was a polemical essay on the gains achieved under the system of comercio libre or Spanish "free trade." Like Basadre, Quirós believed that free trade was an essential policy if Spain and Spanish America were to continue to develop. In addition, Quirós observed that because of the Napoleonic wars Spain had a largely devastated economy. If she was to regain her economic health, he concluded, it was essential to have capital with which to rebuild her factories and therefore commerce seemed the most likely source of these funds. Besides, he observed, a return to restrained trade would only help to spur the smuggling activity carried on by foreign interlopers, most notably the British. He pointed out that restrained trade did far greater damage to the Spanish economy because of Spanish American merchants, especially those in New Spain, were able to receive goods through the contraband trade. Quirós consequently reported that if free trade were continued the profits would naturally go to Spanish merchants and mercantile firms.[25] While the restoration of the monarchy did return much of the former controls, trade remained largely unaltered after Ferdinand VII's return. By 1817 the most pressing problem confronting Bourbon Mexico was the ongoing insurrections which had continued, with spurts and starts, since 1810.

The ongoing rebellion consequently became the backdrop of the second Quirós report of 1817. His Report on the Condition of New Spain was a detailed examination of the Mexican economy from 1804 until 1817. Quirós observed that New Spain was a nation under siege. The insurrection had helped to spur banditry throughout late Bourbon Mexico. Because of the continuing rebellion Quirós claimed that the mining industry had been severely effected. Many mines were either abandoned or flooded because of the attacks carried out by the insurgents. With bandits and rebels roaming the countryside many farms and haciendas were sacked and burned to the ground. Mexico, however, was far from complete devastation or economic collapse as of 1817. Quirós presented a picture of the Mexican economy which applauded its resilience and diversity. Royalist Mexico was a rather healthy economy in 1817 although with apparent blemishes.[26] Quirós remained in the secretariat of the Veracruz consulado well after Mexico gained her independence from Spain. Finally in 1824, with the demise of the consulado, Quirós returned to fulltime mercantile activities.

Rebellion during the early nineteenth century undoubtedly affected the Mexican economy, however, far less than formerly presumed. All colonial Mexican historians are acquainted with the exploits of Fathers Hidalgo and

Morelos. Hidalgo's revolt had a much smaller impact on the Mexican economy than that of Morelos because of its short duration.[27] The Morelos rebellion, in comparison, had a much more profound affect on the economy although far less than one would anticipate. In essence, because Morelos controlled a relatively small part of the viceroyalty, his impact on the Mexican economy was regional rather than national. Eventually, Morelos was captured and executed like his predecessor, Father Hidalgo. Thereupon the insurrection and its leadership was left in disaray.[28] In 1815, immediately after Morelos was executed, Colonel Juan Camargo y Cavallero of the Spanish Royal Corps of Engineers, wrote a report to military and civil authorities in Madrid outlining his observations concerning the effects of the insurrections in the late Mexican colony. He found a Mexican economy still largely intact although still under siege. Camargo was rather optimistic about the capabilities of the army of New Spain and did seem seem particularly alarmed by the continuing insurrections. In general, he echoed the sentiments of all Spanish officials serving in the late Bourbon Mexico.[29]

With the restoration of the Ferdinand VII to the Spanish throne in late 1814 the colonial government again asserted the full weight of its authority. Viceroy Don Félix María Calleja waged a merciless war of attrition against the insurgents which culminated in the execution of Morelos. By 1816 Calleja had entirely pacified the viceroyalty. Strain, however, could be observed among the colonial elites. They felt disenfranchised by Spanish authority. The colonial ethos in fact had been shattered by the events of the late eighteenth and early nineteenth centuries. The colonial government therefore could no longer rely on the political unity of the Mexican elites to support the patrimonial state.[30] In September 1816, Don Juan Ruíz de Apodaca, the Conde de Venadito, was appointed as viceroy of New Spain. While central Mexico remained pacified, portions of southern Mexico were already embroiled in civil war once he arrived in Mexico City. By 1819 Apodaca was writing to officials in Madrid, complaining about the activities of the insurgents throughout New Spain. Of prime concern to Apodaca was the deterioration of the Mexican economy. In letters sent between July and December 1819 the viceroy observed that the rebels had made great headway and were in the process of destroying the Mexican economy. The mines of New Spain no longer produced enough specie to keep the viceregal government sufficiently funded. *Hacendados* abandoned their livestock to the insurgents as a consequence of their fear of losing their lives. Viceroy Apodaca feared that if this condition persisted the Mexican economy would eventually be in ruin.[31] Still, the rebel forces could not achieve total victory. They therefore continued to rely on banditry and ambushes to bring the colonial government down. As of 1819, however, they could not succeed in their goal of ending Spanish rule in Mexico.

It is ironic that it was Ferdinand VII and Agustín de Iturbide who contributed the most toward Mexican Independence. Ferdinand returned to Spain in late 1814 determined to restore Spain's grandeur under the auspices of an absolutist or autocratic monarch. The king nonetheless could not immediately impose his program without possibly precipitating a civil war. The Spanish elites had enjoyed new freedoms in the juntas established in his absence. And they also had fought and shed their blood to return him to his throne. But Ferdinand merely waited for the right time to strike his blow for absolutist authority. He abolished the 1812 Constitution in early 1815 and branded anyone who opposed him a traitor. Hundreds of men were imprisoned in the aftermath of this action. We may conclude that this action also gave new life to the rebel cause in New Spain and throughout Spanish America. Continuing strife in the New World drained the Spanish crown of much needed finances and in January 1820 a contingent of troops destined for Spanish America revolted. Within a few months they forced Ferdinand to restore the 1812 Constitution.[32]

Meanwhile events moved ahead in New Spain. Agustín de Iturbide, who had taken to the field against the insurgents earlier on, joined the rebel cause. The newly established Spanish *cortés* rejected Mexican pleas for autonomy and in February 1821 he issued his own compromise --the Plan of Iguala. Both insurgents and loyalist leaders endorsed Iturbide's proposal. The basic tenets are well known to all Mexican historians and therefore there is no need to repeat them in the present study. The Plan, in essence, put the nails into the coffin of Spanish rule in Mexico. Within seven months of its publication the colonial government collapsed and it was replaced by a new government headed by Iturbide.[33]

To the end the colonial government had insisted on a patrimonial state dominated by Spaniards. No mestizo had ever served as a viceroy and very few had achieved high social status. Moreover in its nearly three centuries of Spanish rule only two creoles had ever served as viceroy, both of whom were noblemen. Throughout the late colonial period the government in New Spain followed a program of increasing centralization. By 1800 nearly every facet of the Mexican economy was affected by the actions of the patrimonial state. During the early eighteenth century, economic thought was considered a tool of the state. In essence, the Bourbon monarchy encouraged the development of economic theory so long as it increased their wealth and power. Economic reform clearly resulted from the theories of Spanish economists during the course of the eighteenth century. The Enlightenment, at least in Spain, sustained the state rather than overturning it. Spanish economic studies did encourage similar intellectual inquiry in the New World. Examples are the studies of Alzate, Basadre, and Quirós. Economic policy, however, was still within the grasp of bureaucrats at the beginning of the nineteenth century. Bureaucrats, such as Revillagigedo and Branciforte, encouraged economic reform primarily because it enhanced their power and that of the patrimonial state.

The French Revolution had a great impact on events in colonial Mexico although not immediate. In 1793 Spain became engaged in a war with Revolutionary France and was subsequently forced to sign a humiliating peace treaty. This event in itself did not cause much concern in Madrid. However, wars cost money and this particular war cost a great deal of money. Henceforth Bourbon finances were in disaray. In addition, after Charles IV agreed to the treaty terms, Great Britain declared war against Spain. From 1796 to 1802 Spain was effectively cutoff from her overseas possessions. This event only worsened the crumbling finances of the Spanish Bourbons. To avert a collapse of the empire Charles IV was forced to authorize the colonists to trade with neutral shipping. Merchants in the Spanish colonies applauded this policy because their wealth grew tremendously. This action later became a seed of discontent when Charles IV and then Ferdinand VII tried to revoke it. Still, Spain's finances continued to worsen. To remedy the fiscal condition the crown enacted the Royal Law of Consolidation in 1798 and then applied it to New Spain in 1804. Consolidation and the increased taxation of the late colonial epoch became a seed which festered and ultimately was used as a pretext for independence. Mexico, however, remained a largely loyal colony until the events of the early 1800s forced the Mexican colony into a reorientation away from Spain.[34]

Napoleon's invasion of the Iberian peninsula became a catalyst which eventually led to Mexican Independence. Ferdinand VII was imprisoned after Bonaparte invaded Spain and the Spanish empire then found itself without a monarch. Colonial officials continued to carry out daily administration, however, without a king they acted only in his name and not through his direction. In 1810 cries of discontent reached a zenith and Father Hidalgo took to the field of battle against maladministration. Both the Hidalgo and Morelos Revolts failed because they represented lower class aspirations rather than the colonial elites who actually controlled the destiny of the colony. Ferdinand VII's restoration and abolition of the 1812 Constitution destroyed the colonial ethos. Spanish Americans and more importantly colonial merchants found these actions as tantamount to breaking a contract. The colonial elites thus considered these actions irksome because they had financed Ferdinand's restoration and also had helped to restore the Hispanic economy. Mexican colonists were also affected by the liberal economic policies advocated by Adam Smith, Vicente Basadre, and José María Quirós. The rejection of their autonomy proposal in 1820 before the Spanish cortes became the last crack in the colonial ethos. Thereupon both rebels and colonial elites combined to bring about the fall of Royal government in New Spain. Spanish officials realized by 1821 that Spain no longer had the strength to retain its empire. In reality, colonial government in Bourbon Mexico collapsed from within.[35]

At Independence a backlash arose against the patrimonial state established by the Spaniards. Iturbide's empire lasted less than three years. Almost immediately after Independence discontent surfaced in response to Iturbide's strongman rule. Mexicans surely did not want to return to a form of Spanish rule. Mexico consequently entered into a new phase of its history. Between 1821 and 1876 Mexico became embroiled in a series of civil wars over the question over centralism versus federalism. While most Mexicans accepted economic liberalism at the beginning of the nineteenth century, conflict continued throughout the century over Mexico's form of government. Porfirio Díaz gained power in 1876 and reasserted the patrimonial state in political affairs. Only friends and allies of the Díaz regime received government posts. Indeed a case can be made that the Mexican Revolution actually resulted in the reassertion of the patrimonial state in economic affairs. Nonetheless colonial forms and institutions have continued to exist throughout the course of Mexican history and still persist to the presentday.

CHAPTER X

CONTEMPORARY MEXICO AND PATRIMONIALISM: THE HISPANIC LEGACY RESTORED?

Mexican history and historiography is frought with many contradictions. In the early twentieth century, Mexico was embroiled in yet another of its many political strifes. In 1910 Francisco Madero embarked on a program "to bring democracy to Mexico." Madero represented the underlying discontent surfacing in the declining years of the Díaz dictatorship. Yet at one time Díaz had represented and championed the cause of order and progress. Throughout the early stages of the nineteenth century, Mexico witnessed many civil wars and even interventions by both the United States and France. Turmoil was a constant occurrence in post-independence Mexico. When Porfirio Díaz came to the presidency during the 1870s, he came to the Mexican people as a national hero and as a champion of economic progress. Very quickly after assuming the Mexican presidency he developed a patrimonial state. Those who supported Don Porfirio received the fruits and rewards from the bounty of the Mexican countryside. Diaz, however, did not try to address the increasing discontent in Mexico, especially among the Mexican peasantry. To control the masses he used terror and appeased the Mexican elites with the proceeds from capitalism and industrialization. Soon, however, the Mexican intelegensia and landed elite questioned the soundness of the Díaz regime. Foreign capital controlled much of the Mexican economy by 1910 and social conditions continued to deteriorate in the face of the expansion of capitalism.[1]

Mexico celebrated the centennial of the Grito de Dolores in 1910 and on the service Mexico appeared to be very peaceful and prosperous. But this facade soon crumbled. In late November 1910 Madero crossed the border, where he had been in exile, and thereupon shot off the first salvo of the Mexican Revolution. After a slow start his insurrection gained steam and in the following May forced Díaz's resignation. Madero, however, was not an ardent revolutionary. Indeed, he only really wanted to restore nineteenth century constitutionalsim to Mexico. But events precluded such a mild remedy for Mexico's many problems. He was never really able to assert his authority. From the outset of the Madero presidency Mexico lacked a viable political concensus. The Mexican elites branded him a radical who wanted to deprive them of the wealth achieved under the Díaz regime. On the other hand, the activists or revolutionaries wanted far greater social, political, and economic reform than what Madero could offer. Madero consequently became an embattled president--hated and maligned by both sides.[2]

The second phase of the Mexican Revolution got underway in 1913. In that year, one of Madero's generals, Victoriano Huerta, allied himself with the silent yet powerful *porfiristas* and staged a coup d'état. Madero was killed under mysterious circumstances and Huerta tried to restore the strongman rule so recognizable with the Díaz regime. The revolutionary movement, largely from the north, was shocked by the events in Mexico City and soon took to the field against the infamous Huerta regime. The names of Carranza, Villa, Zapata, Obregón, and Calles are all well known to students and scholars of modern Mexican history. The state which eventually emerged from the ashes of the Mexican Revolution remains a largely unresearched topic. In reality, what actually emerged was a patrimonial state akin to that of the late colonial period. The patrimonial state of the twentieth century, however, was far different in goals. This state became a catalyst for social, political, and economic change in twentieth century Mexico. Nevertheless it did not become fully developed until the 1930s.[3]

The Mexican Revolution became and is the most important event in the twentieth century. It had a profound effect upon what we call contemporary Mexico. Between 1910 and 1920 Mexico underwent the severest form of chaos--civil war. A direct impact of the revolution surfaced into two distinct areas. First, the population declined drastically from the affects of the civil war. Although an accurate census is not available, many historians claim that as many as two million people perished in the Mexican Revolution. Second, and probably more importantly, the Mexican economy was nearly wrecked because of the destruction and anarchy wrought by the revolutionary period. Indeed, the economy still suffers from the events of this period.[4] For instance, corn, which is the principal staple of the Mexican populace, experienced a drastic decline during the Revolution. Its production shrunk to a mere 2 million tons in 1920--a level not significantly above that of the late eighteenth century. Nearly every sector of the Mexican economy was affected in a similar manner. Still, however, government revenues continued to rise. But this increase cannot be attributed to the efficiency of the Mexican government but rather to the burgeoning of the Mexican oil industry. Oil production grew from a mere 3.6 million barrels in 1910 to nearly 194 million barrels in 1921. By the end of the Mexican Revolution the nation was the world's third largest producer of petroleum.[5]

Sinews of the patrimonial state grew even during the civil war. In September 1914 Carranza issued a decree which barred from candidacy any individual who opposed the Constitutionalist cause. Moreover many of Carranza's ideas concerning Mexican society and politics were incorporated into the 1917 Constitution. Carranza advocated a more moderate course in reforming Mexican society. On the other hand, the radicals, as they were so-named, opposed the Carranza clique. In essence, however, little or no differences emerged among these two factions. They differed in methods rather than aims. The radicals nonetheless wanted to establish an activist state--a patrimonial state. They believed that a centralized state was much more capable in initiating social and economic change. The resulting constitution, while temperate in composition, attacked some of the evils which plagued Mexico throughout the life of the Diaz dictatorship. The Church was deprived of its dominance in education and its control of wealth. Harkening back to the Spanish period, the Constitution reserved to the state all sub-soil rights and also recognized the legality of *ejidos*. Ultimately, Carranza found much to quarrel with in the constitution drafted by the Convention. Instead of creating a schism, however, he decided to return to Spanish tradition. He consequently only enforced those provisions which he agreed with and would spur Mexican development.[6]

While most of the delegates at Querétaro believed that the Constitution would cure Mexico's ills overnight, the process was long and tortuous. Strongman rule characterized much of the 1920s. One man surprisingly changed the course of Mexican history during the 1930s. That man was Lázaro Cárdenas and contributed the most toward the twentieth century Mexican state. Cárdenas tied the emerging patrimonial state to the myth or creed of the Mexican Revolution. He was elected to the Mexican presidency in 1934 and thereupon embarked on a program to centralize the revolutionary government. In that year he also began his program "to socialize education." The Ministry of Education consequently became an onclave of socialism. More importantly Cárdenas made education an issue of patriotism. Teachers were no longer just educators but were henceforth social advocates and leaders.[7] Next Cárdenas attacked the landed elites by expropriating their lands and especially those held by foreigners. By the end of his presidential term in 1940, Cárdenas had expropriated and redistributed some 17,000 hectares. Cárdenas, in this program, relied on the time tested institution of the _ejido_. His confidence in the institution was not ill founded. Agricultural production between 1939 and 1941 rose higher than before the onslaught of the Mexican Revolution. Indeed, the Mexican peasants enjoyed a higher standard-of-living in 1940 in comparison to their 1910 income level. Nutrition levels rose and as a consequence mortality rates improved as well during the Cárdenas era. Cárdenas utilized the patrimonial state to improve agricultural production and it did increase tremendously. Cárdenas' agricultural reforms were probably the most successful of his presidency.

The Mexican Revolution increased nationalist feelings in Mexico and Cárdenas used it to accomplish some of his social goals. He therefore focused attention on the exploitation borne by foreigners and foreign companies in Mexico. He stated to the masses that foreign control of the Mexican economy was the chief reason for their problems. Using this rhetoric, Cárdenas had delineated a real threat. In fact, prior to the Mexican Revolution, foreign business interests nearly owned the country. As of 1914 United States and French businessmen owned more of Mexico than did the Mexican populace. Oil consequently became a focus of the Cárdenas regime. In March 1938, he issued a decree expropriating all oil company lands in Mexico controlled by foreigners. The oil companies cried out against this action by the Mexican government and branded Cárdenas a Marxist. They called the whole process illegal and thereupon decided to take action against Cárdenas and the Mexican people. Hoping to bring about an economic crisis, the American oil companies refused to allow their oil tankers to land on Mexican soil. These companies hoped that they could force the Cárdenas regime to rescind its decree or if not, then participate an intervention by the United States.[8]

The Cárdenas regime and its successors were not anti-capitalist. On the contrary, they used the Mexican state to promote capitalism in Mexico. Cárdenas, however, had inherited a country which still suffered from the effects of the Revolution. As a consequence of the weak Mexican state and economy, Cárdenas had imposed a patrimonial state. The vehicle for patrimonialism became the Partido Revolucionario Institucional (PRI). In essence, by creating this one-party system, Cárdenas and succeeding presidents were able to fashion a new oligarchy or ruling order. Loyalty to the Mexican Revolution through the PRI since 1940 has remained the only and principal route of political mobility. Much of the current criticism from political scientists and historians centers around the authoritarian aspects of the Mexican system. These researchers seem a bit ethnocentric in their analysis of contemporary Mexico. In reality, Mexico is neither an authoritarian nor democratic state.[9] It is basically a patrimonial state not unlike that fashioned by the Bourbons at least from the standpoint of the innerworkings of politics. Samuel P. Huntington has shown that there are many variants of democracy; that each society has its own concept of democracy and freedom. In most developing nations a centralized government has been a requisite to promote rapid economic growth and progress.[10]

Modern or contemporary Mexico is clearly dominated by the inclusive PRI party and the legend of the Mexican Revolution. During the late colonial period a similar relationship existed under the Spanish Bourbons. The king therefore represented the inclusive state much like that of presentday Mexico. For almost four centuries of colonial rule, most Mexicans felt content in being part of the larger inclusive Spanish empire. The present Mexican state has replaced the viceroy of colonial times with a president who is chosen by the ruling PRI party. Mexico's president, like the viceroy of the colonial era, is picked or selected on the basis of past appointments and on his loyalty to the PRI party; not unlike the loyalty required by a sovereign.[11] The Mexican president is at the apex of the Mexican government much like the viceroy of the colonial period. Neither, however, was or is omnipotent. Each president's decisions and policies are tempered by the PRI itself and various interest groups represented in it. In the case of the colonial viceroy, his actions were restrained by crown policy and by the fact that all colonial subjects could seek redress directly from the monarch. All colonial officials, including the viceroy, were subjected to an official review of their actions in office known as a <u>residencía</u>. A contemporary illustration of this traditional process is the official review which occurs after each president's term.[12]

Both the Bourbon and PRI concept of government follows a corporatist theory of society. The Bourbon monarchy and its colonial officialdom believed in a hierarchical form of government. So does the presentday Mexican government controlled by the PRI. Government serves four basic functions under corporatist system. (1) regulates class conflict (2) implement political and economic decisions (3) rationalizes political procedures and (4) effectively executes the mechanisms of political and economic control.[13] On these lines of inquiry, the PRI serves as a stabilizing factor as did the Bourbon monarchy and the colonial bureaucracy during the late colonial period. Both the PRI and Bourbon reformers are and were advocates of progress. More importantly, however, both viewed and view stability (order) as a requisite for progress.

As in colonial New Spain, contemporary Mexico is a highly stratified society. The top twenty percent of the populace controls in excess of sixty percent of the wealth whereas the bottom twenty percent controls only four percent of the wealth.[14] Mexico consequently is controlled by a ruling oligarchy or class as it was during the late colonial period. In Bourbon Mexico all of the important government posts were held by Spaniards. Spaniards were the primary _camarilla_ (clique) in the late eighteenth and early nineteenth centuries. Wealthy creoles were allowed to serve in the second tier of influence and power. They served basically in provincial and local political entities such as the *cabildo* and *ayuntamiento*. Class therefore played a pivotal role in the stratification of colonial Mexican society as it does today.[15] As was true in late colonial society, social mobility is controlled by education as well as occupation. In terms of the bureaucracy of contemporary Mexico, it is primarily the economists trained at the National Autonomous University in Mexico City who control the apparatus of government. Indeed, this phenomena in Mexican politics is even more apparent with regard to cabinet posts. As of 1980, six out of ten cabinet posts were held by economists.[16] Economists, in addition, have a great deal of influence within the hierarchy of the PRI. An analysis of late Bourbon Mexico reveals a very similar relationship. Viceroys, such as the Conde de Revillagigedo, Marqués de Branciforte, and Miguel José de Azanza, were all well educated. The intendants in addition were well educated and in many cases were trained in technical sciences such as engineering and political economy.[17] It is natural, however, that in both cases the better educated should predominate in the bureaucratic ranks given the persistent push for economic progress in the course of Mexican history.

Control is an essential commodity for any political system. Tradition continues to guide the leaders of contemporary Mexico. The principal mechanism of political control and stability is that of cooptation. Under this system interest groups and political cliques are traded concessions in return for their loyalty and support to the PRI.[18] During the late colonial period cooptation was the cornerstone of Spanish colonial policy. True, the crown could and did use force when cooptation failed. Force, however, often engendered ill will toward the colonial government and the Spanish crown avoided using force unless absolutely necessary. The "fueros" established in Spanish Mexico are an illustration of the colonial form of cooptation. Another form of cooptation during the late colonial period was the semi-autonomous bodies such as the consulados and gremios. Even with the implementation of the intendant ordinances in 1786 lower government posts continued to be retained by creoles and the colonial elites. While desiring a much more centralized and activist state, the Bourbon reformers also recognized that they had to play by the rules established in the preceding centuries of Spanish rule. Ultimately, it was the inability of the crown to mediate various interests in late colonial Mexico which influenced and led to the demise of Spanish rule.[19]

A cornerstone of the Bourbon program was that of economic progress. By the mid-eighteenth century the reinvigoration of the Mexican economy became of crucial importance. By the 1770s New Spain provided the largest sums to finance colonial administration as well as financing some of Spain's debt. The Spanish Bourbons therefore decided to assist this continuing development by restructuring the government. The intendancies were introduced into New Spain to increase the power of the crown and the patrimonial state.[20] They also reformed the offices of the Royal Exchequer to bring in more funds to the coffers of New Spain. More importantly, however, the crown advocated and installed an activist state. For instance, the viceregency of Revillagigedo was a period of great progress. Revillagigedo issued decrees which reorganized the marketplaces. He also utlized the special skills of the Royal Corps of Engineers to improve the infrastructure of New Spain.[21] Economic liberalism was promoted but within the confines of a centralized patrimonial state. The great strides made in the Mexican economy clearly assisted in increasing the stability of the viceroyalty.[22] Spain's own problems and the Napoleonic wars also helped in dismantling the colonial ethos. It was Ferdinand VII's intransigence and inability to coopt discontented elements which ultimately led to the schism between Spain and Spanish America.

The PRI, since the days of Cárdenas, has tried to expand its base of support. Their principal tool has been the promotion of economic development and social change. Mexico's economy has expanded markedly during the twentieth century. However, it has not grown as fast as the population, nor has it resolved the maldistribution of wealth. Increased urbanization, particularly in Mexico City, has intensified Mexico's economic problems and has produced instability.[23] To confront contemporary Mexico's many problems the ruling elites of the PRI have increasingly relied on the acceleration of economic growth. Technocracy consequently has become a byproduct of this drive for rapid economic development. Economists, the primary technocrats of contemporary Mexico, now control most of the political and policy apparatus of the Mexican state. Similar to the state fashioned in the late colonial period, the modern Mexican state has adopted a semi-socialized economy to prevent foreign or capitalist domination. Certain sectors of the Mexican economy are totally controlled by the government such as public utilities, mining, petroleum, and other key areas. During the late colonial period the colonial government dominated certain sectors of the economy and the Spanish crown even created monopolies to restrain nascent capitalism. The crown, however, was motivated by a more important concern; that of increasing the power of the patrimonial state and increasing the size of New Spain's revenues.[24]

As we have noted previously the Bourbon monarchy and the PRI have resorted to coercion when all else has failed.

Both states nevertheless have preferred cooptation rather than violence. Most prudent governments follow this course of action. Examples of the use of force are found both in colonial and modern Mexican history. In 1767 the crown forcibly expelled the Jesuits from New Spain over the protestations of the population. Again in 1766 the crown used force to quell a labor revolt in the mines of Real del Monte. Probably the best example of the use of force in the colonial period occurred during the Mexican Wars of Independence. The Army of New Spain waged a merciless war against the insurgents often killing civilians.[25] As Paul Vanderwood has observed quite recently disorder is a byproduct of rapid development. Porfirio Díaz created the Rurales primarily as a tool of the Mexican state. They were used to crush dissent and at the same time quelled banditry. Indeed, while being a personal security force for Díaz they were also a catalyst to Mexican development.[26] Even the PRI have used force and violence at various times because no other remedy existed. During the 1920s, for instance, the Revolutionary Army was utilized to crush the Cristero Rebellion. Again, in 1968, the Army was used to crush a possible revolt in Mexico City.[27] No state whether democratic or authoritarian can allow a challenge to authority to go unchecked. In essence, the state has a life of its own.

The Spanish tradition is a lasting influence on modern Mexican history. Many historians and other social scientists may disagree with this conclusion but the historical facts speak for themselves. The government of both contemporary and colonial Mexico is and was primarily a patrimonial state. It is clear that the government of late colonial Mexico was much more activist than in previous eras. The Bourbon monarchy pursued centralization and patrimonialism primarily in response to the economic revolution in eighteenth century Europe. A patrimonial state seemed the only viable type of government which could properly direct the Mexican economy and at the same time sustain the Bourbon monarchy. It is consequently only natural that the state born out of the Mexican Revolution is mainly patrimonial in structure. Contemporary Mexico is essentially ruled by an oligarchy of technocrats whose primary goal is economic development and modernization. As Lesley Byrd Simpson stated so long ago, Mexico is a land of many contrasts and traditions. Patrimonialism is one of these time tested traditions left by Spanish rule. The society and politics of modern Mexico, while unlike Bourbon Mexico, has many of the attributes of its colonial legacy. The patrimonial state is probably the most enduring legacy of Spanish rule.

Western historians and political scientists have tended until recently to judge contemporary Mexico on the basis of the British heritage of democracy and ignoring the Spanish tradition. Democracy has become a panacea for most Western historians and any deviation from the model has been branded as authoritarianism. How can we judge on the basis of our heritage? Spanish rule was both authoritarian and paternalistic. The present Mexican state is an outgrowth of this tradition. Because of the chaos accompanying the nineteenth and early twentieth centuries, the oligarchy which rules Mexico has sacrificed democracy in favor of stability. Contemporary Mexico consequently reflects the course of Mexican history and continues to retain shadows of her colonial past.

CONCLUSION

The foregoing study has focused upon two major themes. First, the Bourbon economic reforms created a great spurt in the late eighteenth century and colonial bureaucrats played an essential role in the development and implementation of these reforms. Part One of this monograph answers how these policies spurred significant economic development in late colonial New Spain and how the Mexican bureaucracy utilized policy to encourage economic expansion. Part Two of this present work describes and analyzes the growth of the patrimonial state during the late colonial period. Indeed, both the successes and failures of the bureaucracy must be weighed according to the philosophy of the patrimonial state. By the late eighteenth century, the colonial bureaucracy played a vital if not essential role in directing economic policies.

Succession of the Bourbon dynasty at the beginning of the eighteenth century not only brought a change in Spain's ruling house, but also the propagation of new "enlightened" ideas. The Age of Reason had a strong practical bent. Spanish economists developed reform policy recommendations which echoed enlightenment concepts. Eighteenth century ministers adopted many of the proposals advocated by economists to revive Spanish overseas commerce. Between 1765 and 1789, the crown authorized a system of _comercio libre_ for the Indies. Like the peninsulars, the Americans praised the progressive and enlightened reforms enacted by the Bourbons. Colonial bureaucrats were attracted to the economic ideas which the crown promulgated and they implemented programs which were in tune with those policies embraced by the Bourbon monarchy.

In Mexico, viceroys and intendants developed a group of far-reaching economic policies to accentuate the pace of economic development. The viceroys within the Mexican setting were the primary officials responsible for ensuring that Mexico's economy expanded. Probably the most notable late eighteenth century viceroys were Antonio María Bucareli, the second Conde de Revillagigedo, and the Marqués de Branciforte.

Development of public works was an essential part of the viceregal government's promotion of commercial and economic development. Construction of road networks throughout Mexico was fundamental in guaranteeing that Mexico's produce was delivered to market. Continued development of New Spain's defenses by the Royal Corps of Engineers guaranteed that the commercial centers would never be vulnerable to attack. The naval forces of San Blas serviced both the trade with Manila and California.

The introduction of street-lighting in Mexico City reduced the crime rate and encouraged increased commercial activity.

Late colonial viceroys increasingly became advocates of commercialized agriculture and tried to introduce new crops which would be conducive to commercial expansion. Most of these attempts were unsuccessful because of the limited Mexican market where tradition influenced consumption patterns. Viceregal official applauded the publication of pamphlets encouraging the utilization of crop rotation and other signs of modernization. Crop rotation, for instance, increased the crop yields significantly in some areas of Mexico. In addition, the viceregal government promoted the use of irrigation systems in those locations where rainfall was limited. The markets for commercial agricultural products were the large urban centers. Cochineal and indigo were the primary agricultural commodities traded in the overseas markets. Between 1779 and 1816, the value of agricultural production in New Spain grew from a mere 19 million pesos to 138 million pesos. Mexican agriculture was favorably influenced by enlightened viceregal policies, and in terms of the wealth generated, was the most important sector of the economy.

Mexican industrial policies were tied to those policies adopted in the peninsula to expand Spanish industry. The primary vehicle for expanding Mexican industry was the development of technology which the late viceregal governments continually encouraged. The larger markets for industrial goods resulting from the increased incomes of those involved in agriculture and commerce also helped Mexican industry. Late colonial viceroys attempted to direct the evolution of Mexican industry by holding regular meetings with prominent industrialists to discuss industrialization and possible policy shifts by the viceregal government. Most industry in Mexico was located near the large urban centers where the demand for industrial products was largest. Textile production was clearly the principal commodity produced in Mexico's *obrajes*.

Both the internal and external trade of Mexico grew significantly in the late eighteenth century under the influence of enlightened Caroline and viceregal reforms. *Comercio libre* was extended to New Spain in 1789 by Charles IV and thereafter aided in expanding Mexico's international trade. Commercial expansion was a primary focus of the late colonial viceroys. Revillagigedo stands out among eighteenth century colonial officials in promoting increases in both domestic and international trade. Creation of two new *consulados* in Veracruz and Guadalajara increased competition among the Mexico City merchants. As the foregoing study has shown, commercial interaction through Veracruz grew tremendously in the late Bourbon century, expanding from 21.5 million pesos in 1792 to nearly 60.3 million pesos in 1802.

By the end of the eighteenth century New Spain had become the most prosperous and wealthy of the Spanish American viceroyalties. Economic affairs claimed a great share of the crown's and colonial bureaucracy's attention. Government aid, legislation, and leadership stimulated production. In nearly every economic endeavor remarkable advances were achieved. Legislation was drafted with the sincere intent to improve the quality of products and to encourage legitimate business, industry, mining, and farming. Economic statistics of the late eighteenth century attest to the general prosperity existing in the late Mexican colony.

Charles III was probably the most capable of the Bourbon monarchs in the area of economic affairs. He promoted technical training and rewarded contributions to economic development. Caroline economic reforms and policies constituted a major reversal of the role of the crown and the colonial bureaucracy in economic matters. No longer did the government take a passive role in economic development. While the Hapsburgs had insisted upon adherence to imperial economic doctrine, the Bourbon reformers were much more interested in efficiency and the accomplishment of crown objectives. In light of the increased ability to direct policy, the colonial administrators increasingly became active participants in the promotion of commerce, agriculture, and industry. The success of the government's economic programs rested upon the efficiency of colonial bureaucrats and the enterprise of the colonial merchants.

Patrimonialism was neither an alien nor new concept to late colonial Mexico. From the outset of Spanish rule, the Spanish crown had built a patrimonial state yet not to the degree of the Spanish Bourbons. The adoption of such a structure during the late eighteenth century transformed the Mexican colony into a highly centralized society. The Gálvez Visitation was the catalyst of the political reforms instituted in late colonial Mexico and the remainder of the Spanish empire. During his visitation he made recommendations to introduce intendants into New Spain. Gálvez, however, was not able to establish intendancies in Bourbon Mexico immediately. Charles III was not sure of the efficacy of such a radical departure in colonial administration. Gálvez subsequently returned to Spain in 1771 and continued to pursue his career and greater centralization in colonial politics. Moreover, Charles III placed great confidence in Gálvez's abilities and in 1776 named him the Minister of the Indies.

Don José de Gálvez was a strong supporter of the patrimonial state. Beginning in 1776 he began to press for the introduction of intendants and intendancies into the Spanish empire. Yet Gálvez was unable to fulfill his dream of establishing intendancies in New Spain until 1786; a year before his departure from the Ministry of the Indies. Eventually Charles III perceived that centralization was the best way to improve colonial administration. All of the intendants dispatched to late Bourbon Mexico were Spaniards and specially trained for their posts. Because of his power and prestige, Gálvez was able to appoint many of his friends and relatives into these posts. The second Conde de Revillagigedo, who served between 1789 and 1794, was the viceroy who fully implemented the intendant decrees. Revillagigedo consequently defined the political and economic functions of the intendants, giving them far-reaching powers, particularly in the economic arena.

The intendant ordinances were also a catalyst for other branches of the colonial bureaucracy. Finances were of crucial importance to the late colonial viceroys as well as the Bourbon monarchs. As the economy expanded during the late eighteenth century so too did the Royal Exchequer and its subsidiary branches. Revillagigedo was responsible for the great growth of the *Real aduana* during the 1790s. They grew from a mere 300 officials to nearly 500 officers by the end of his administration. Revillagigedo and Charles IV expanded the operations and powers of the *Real aduana*. In the aftermath of the Gálvez Visitation, the crown authorized the construction of additional customhouses. This program continued abait throughout the remainder of the colonial period. Throughout the 1780s and 1790s the Royal Corps of Engineers were utilized to construct and repair customhouses in addition to their regular military duties. By 1800 New Spain had twenty some customhouses spread across the breadth of the viceroyalty to facilitate expanded trade and commerce.

Other branches of the Royal Exchequer expanded during the late colonial epoch in response to the growth of the Mexican economy and patrimonial state. Mexico City, quite naturally, was the site of the headquarters for exchequer operations and affairs. The offices of the Royal Exchequer were located directly adjacent to the viceregal palace. As a consequence of the Gálvez Visitation and the Caroline reforms, monopolies were created and expanded to increase Bourbon finances. Spain needed ever increasing sums of money to sustain the empire and the monarchy, especially after 1793. The gunpowder, playing-card, *pulque*, and lottery monopolies provided much needed funds to support viceregal and crown activities in the late Mexican colony. New Spain became an integral source of surplus funds and by 1800 was providing some 11 million pesos to support the Spanish empire. The financial bureaucracies in late colonial Mexico were a keystone of imperial politics because they strengthened royal power and assisted in the growth of the patrimonial state.

The second Conde de Revillagigedo stands out among the viceroys of the late colonial period. He was an ardent supporter of the intendant system and other centralization schemes undertaken by the Caroline monarchs. Revillagigedo's fame, however, rests primarily on his role as a promoter of economic development. He strongly believed in maintaining the colonial ethos as well as strengthening Spanish rule in Mexico. He greatly expanded the colonial bureaucracy to meet the enlarged role and power of the viceregal government. Revillagigedo utilized the intendants and other colonial officials as chroniclers of the Mexican economy; sending them out to collect and maintain economic data. To promote comercio libre within the Mexican colony, he issued a wide variety of decrees to improve the infrastructure. He improved local commerce by drafting a set of model ordinances for New Spain's many public marketplaces. In addition, the Conde de Revillagigedo promoted road repair and construction.

As an ardent monarchist, Viceroy Revillagigedo understood and believed in a strong central government. Indeed, he believed that without such a government the Mexican economy could not develop at a rapid pace. To this late colonial viceroy, New Spain was a patrimony of the Caroline monarchs and as such the viceroyalty should assist in financing the Spanish empire. His successors, such as the Marqués de Branciforte and Miguel José de Azanza, pursued his programs and policies with varying degrees of success. Many programs, however, had to be curtailed because of their limited success. For instance, the promotion of lino and cañamo production never really got off to a smooth start. In essence, it is an illustration of one of the economic policy failures undertaken in the late Mexican colony. Nonetheless, the saga of the second Conde de Revillagigedo in New Spain illustrates the attempts to promote the patrimonial state and economic development.

Economic thought played an important if not crucial role in transforming both Spain and Spanish America. Spanish economists during the early eighteenth century helped to develop economic policies for the Spanish Indies and eventually influenced the Caroline monarchs into adopting comercio libre as well as the intendant reforms. New Spain was not an intellectual backwater as some historians might have perceived. Intelligent people such as the Conde de Revillagigedo, José Antonio Alzate y Ramírez, Vicente Basadre, and José María Quirós, developed their own theories concerning the development of the Mexican economy. Spain's financial difficulties nonetheless affected the colonial ethos and eventually led to the downfall of the Royalist government in the Mexican colony. The insurrections of the early nineteenth century undoubtedly affected the Mexican economy, however, to what degree.

Spanish policy toward its colonial possessions in the New World ultimately gave impetus to the independence movements.

As of 1821 colonial Mexico no longer relied on Spain and the Bourbon monarchs for direction. Because the Spanish crown and *cortés* refused to grant limited autonomy to New Spain, the colonial ethos of three centuries was shattered. Mexico no longer needed Spanish officials to direct its economy nor to administer the state. Independence ironically came to Mexico in 1821 with hardly a shot being fired. Agustín de Iturbide merely established his own government and used the colonial officialdom to maintain order. In essence, he took over the still intact patrimonial state. Throughout the nineteenth century Mexicans fought over the issue of federalism versus centralism. The state eventually fashioned by Porfirio Díaz was primarily a patrimonial state. He utilized the Mexican bureaucracy he created to achieve his goals of order and progress. The Mexican Revolution initially was a response to the political deprivation of the Díaz regime yet changed later into a struggle over centralism versus federalism.

Madero's successors ultimately were forced to adopt a patrimonial state to achieve their objectives of economic progress and social change. Throughout the 1920s and 1930s the Mexican state grew in its power. It was Lázaro Cárdenas who truly fashioned the modern patrimonial state. Gradually, Cárdenas and his successors increasingly relied on technocrats to achieve their goal of order and progress. Today the Mexican state has entrusted the economic affairs of the nation to university trained economists. Revolutionary Mexico consequently was forced to return to the time tested patrimonial state. Indeed, modern Mexico returned to its colonial roots and the Hispanic tradition. Modern Mexico defies definition as either an authoritarian or democratic nation. The presentday patrimonial state reflects the enduring Spanish or Hispanic legacy. Contemporary Mexico is essentially a Hispanic nation which has clung to many of its Spanish traditions; chief among them being the patrimonial state.

NOTES

Chapter 1

1. Joseph de Veitia Linaje, Norte de la Contratación de las Indias Occidentales (Sevilla: Imprenta de Juan Francisco de Blas, 1672), Book I, Chapter 14, paragraph 11.
2. Clarence H. Haring, Trade and Navigation between Spain and the Indies in the Time of the Hapsburgs (Cambridge: Harvard University Press, 1918), 4-45.
3. Archivo General de las Indias (hereafter cited as AGI), Indiferente General, leg. 542, Proyecto para galeones y flotas del Peru y Nueva España y para navios de registro y avisos que navegaren a ambos reinos, 1720.
4. Richard Herr, The Eighteenth Century Revolution in Spain (Princeton: Princeton University Press, 1958), 120-125; Jacques A. Barbier, "The Culmination of the Bourbon Reforms, 1787-1792," Hispanic American Historical Review 57 (February 1977): 51-60.
5. Elizabeth Fox-Genovese, The Origins of the Physiocracy (Ithaca: Cornell University Press, 1976), 45-66; John H. Parry, The Spanish Seaborne Empire (New York: Alfred A. Knopf, Inc., 1966),282 and 315; Charles Gibson, Spain in America (New York: Harper and Row, Inc., 1966), 166-172
6. Real Academía de la Historía (hereafter cited as RAH), Coleccion Muñoz, Ms. 49, fol. 149.
7. RAH, Coleccion Muñoz, Ms. 49, fol. 150; Marcelo Bitar Letayf, Economistas españoles del siglo XVIII (Madrid: Ediciones Cultura Hispanica, 1968), 97-109.
8. RAH, Coleccion Muñoz, Ms. 49, fol. 150; Clarence H. Haring, The Spanish Empire in America (New York: Harcourt, Brace, and World, Inc., 1963), 318-321.
9. RAH, Coleccion Muñoz, Ms. 49, fol. 151.
10. Ibid.
11. Ricardo Levene, ed., Documentos para la historia Argentina, 7 vols. (Buenos Aires: Compañía Sud-Americana de Billetes de Banco, 1915-1916), 5: 172-187.
12. Bernardo Ward, Proyecto económico, en que se proponen varias providencias dirigidas a promover los intereses de España, con los medios y fondos necesarios para su plantificación (Madrid: Imprenta de J. Ibarra, 1779), 314-319; RAH, Coleccion Muñoz, Ms. 49, fol. 152.
13. John S. Fox, "Antonio de San José Muro: Political Economist of New Spain," Hispanic American Historical Review 21 (August 1941): 410-416.
14. Archivo Histórico de Hacienda (hereafter cited as AHH), Consulado, leg. 1040, exp. 14, Reflexiones sobre el comercio libre de las Américas, 1817.
15. AGI, Indiferente General, leg. 432, Real cédula de 28 de octubre de 1713.

Notes

16. W.N. Hargreaves-Mawdsley, ed. Spain under the Bourbons, 1700-1833: A Collection of Documents (London: Macmillan and Company, 1973), 97-98; Pío Zabala y Lera, España bajo los Borbones, 5 ed. (Barcelona: Editorial Labor, S.A., 1955), 35-42.
17. Hargreaves-Mawdsley, Spain under the Bourbons, 132-134; Charles E. Chapman, A History of Spain (New York: Macmillan Company, 1918), 387.
18. Hargreaves-Mawdsley, Spain under the Bourbons,167.
19. Herbert I. Priestley, José de Gálvez, Visitor-General of New Spain, 1765-1771 (Berkeley: University of California Press, 1916), 25-29.
20. Ibid., 167.
21. Levene, Documentos, 5: 197-198.
22. Ibid., 219-223.
23. Ibid., 249-250.
24. Bitar Letayf, Economistas, 53.
25. Levene, Documentos, 5: 306-310; Guillermo Tardiff, Historia general del comercio exterior mexicano, 2 vols. (México: By the Author, 1968), 1: 107-121.
26. Archivo Histórico Nacional (hereafter cited as AHN), Diversos de Indias, leg. 472, exp. 6, Real decreto de febrero de 1778.
27. Levene, Documentos, 5: 413-414.
28. Levene, Documentos, 6: 3-132; Tardiff, Historia general, 1: 107-121.
29. Álvaro Flórez Estrada, Examen imparcial de las disensiones de la América con España de los medios de su reconciliación y de la prosperidad de todas las naciones (Cádiz: 1812), 66-67.
30. Haring, The Spanish Empire, 321-323.
31. AGI, México, leg. 2505, Real decreto de 28 de febrero de 1789; Miguel Lerdo de Tejada, Comercio exterior de México desde la conquista hasta hoy (México: Impreso de Rafael Rafael, 1853), 19-23; Hemeroteca Nacional de México (hereafter cited as HNM), Gaceta de México, 26 June 1786, Tomo II, 13-26.

Chapter 2

1. Archivo General de la Nación (hereafter cited as AGN), Acordada, vol. 9, exp. 180, Instrucción que deberan observar los tenientes y comisarios del Real Tribunal de la Acordada; AGN, Acordada, vol. 31, exp. 41, Judge Manuel Antonio de Santa María to Revillagigedo II, 26 March 1792.
2. AGN, Virreyes, vol. 26, Carta No. 627 (reservada), Revillagigedo II to Diego Gardoquí, 31 August 1793.
3. Mexico's roads prior to the eighteenth century consisted of those leading to the mining centers of Zacatecas and Guanajuato. See Philip W. Powell, Soldiers,

Indians, and Silver: North America's First Frontier War (Berkeley: University of California Press, 1952; reprint ed., Tempe: Arizona State University, Center for Latin American Studies, 1975), 16-28 and Peter J. Bakewell, Silver Mining and Society in Colonial Mexico: Zacatecas, 1546-1700 (Cambridge: Cambridge University Press, 1971), 20-23.

4. Biblioteca Nacional de Madrid (hereafter cited as BNM), Ms. 477, Descripción de los caminos que desde la plaza de Veracruz se dirigen a Méjico por distintos rumbos, por D. Diego de Panes y Abellan; Carlos Francisco de Croix, Instrucción del Marqués de Croix que deja a sucesor Antonio María Bucareli, ed. Norman F. Martin (México: Editorial Jus, S.A., 1960), 79-80.

5. Don Pedro Alonso O'Crouley, A Description of the Kingdom of New Spain, 1774, trans. and ed. Sean Galvin (San Francisco: John Howell Books, 1972), 43-44.

6. Bernard E. Bobb, The Viceregency of Antonio María Bucareli in New Spain, 1771-1779 (Austin: University of Texas Press, 1962), 115-127; Andrés Cavo, Los tres siglos de Méjico durante el gobierno español hasta la entrada del ejército trigarante (Jalapa: Tipografía de A. Ruíz, 1870), 316-327.

7. AGN, Virreyes, vol. 26, Carta No. 627 (reservada), Revillagigedo II to Gardoquí, 31 August 1793.

8. Don Juan Vicente Güemes, Pacheco, Padilla y Horcasitas, segundo conde de Revilla Gigedo, Instrucción reservada que el conde de Revilla Gigedo dío a sucesor en el mando, Marqués de Branciforte sobre el gobierno de este continente en el tiempo que fué su virrey, 30 de junio de 1794 (México: Imprenta de C. Agustín Guiol, 1831), articles 186-194.

9. Biblioteca Central Militar (hereafter cited as BCM), ms. 2-2-4-7, Ingenieros en México y Filipinas.

10. Miguel José de Azanza, Instrucción reservada que dío el Virrey Don Miguel José de Azanza a sucesor Don Félix Berenquer de Marquina, ed. Ernesto de la Torre (México: Editorial Jus, S.A., 1960), 69; David A. Brading, Miners and Merchants in Bourbon Mexico, 1763-1810 (Cambridge: Cambridge University Press, 1971), 127.

11. Barding, Miners and Merchants, 118.

12. Ibid., 127.

13. Alejandro de Humboldt, Ensayo político sobre el reino de la Nueva España, ed. Juan A. Ortega y Medina (México: Editorial Porrúa, S.A., 1966), 464.

14. BCM, ms. 2-3-4-3, Ingenieros en México y Filipinas; Croix, Instrucción, 81; Janet R. Fireman, The Spanish Royal Royal Corps of Engineers in the Western Borderlands: Instrument of Bourbon Reform, 1764 to 1815 (Glendale, California: Arthur H. Clark Company, 1977), 164.

15. Revilla Gigedo, Instrucción reservada, articles 173-187.
16. Azanza, Instrucción reservada, 69.
17. Clarence N. Guice, "The Consulado of New Spain, 1595-1795" (Ph.D. dissertation, University of California, Berkeley, 1952), 120.
18. Museo Naval (hereafter cited as MN), Reyno de México III, ms. 335, Bando de 26 de noviembre de 1790; O'Crouley, A Description, 29-31.
19. AGN, Virreyes, vol. 26, Carta No. 627 (reservada), Revillagigedo II to Gardoquí, 31 August 1793.
20. MN, Reyno de México III, ms. 335, Bando de 26 de marzo de 1791.
21. BCM, ms. 2-3-4-7, Ingenieros en México y Filipinas; Revilla Gigedo, Instrucción reservada, articles 196-199.
22. James D. Riley, "The Management of the Estates of the Jesuit Colegio Máximo de San Pedro y San Pablo of Mexico City in the Eighteenth Century" (Ph.D. dissertation, Tulane University, 1972), 140-176.
23. AGN, Virreyes, vol. 26, Carta No. 627 (reservada), Revillagigedo II to Gardoquí, 31 August 1793.
24. BCM, ms. 5-3-9-5, Situación en que se hallan todas las provincias del reino de Nueva España fronterizas a la gentilidad en las partes del norte; BNM, ms. 19266, Descripción sucinta de las provincias de Culiacán, Sinaloa, y Sonora; Library of Congress (hereafter cited as LC), Manuscript Division, Peter Force Papers, Series XVIII-C, Item 5, Memorias sobre las provincias del norte de Nueva España, 1799, por Jose Cortés; Max L. Moorhead, New Mexico's Royal Road: Trade and Travel on the Chihuahua Trail (Norman: University of Oklahoma Press, 1958), 32-54.
25. AGN, Virreyes, vol. 26, Carta No. 627 (reservada), Revillagigedo II to Gardoquí, 31 August 1793; David R. Ringrose, "Carting in the Hispanic Word: An Example of Divergent Development," Hispanic American Historical Review 50 (February 1970): 34-41.
26. AGN, Virreyes, vol. 26, Carta No. 627 (reservada), Revillagigedo II to Gardoquí, 31 August 1793; Humboldt, Ensayo politico, 463.
27. Charles Trumbull Hayden Memorial Library, Collection of Eighteenth Century Documents of New Spain (hereafter cited as CECDNS), Carta No. 17, 27 July 1790, fols. 21r-23r, Remite testimonio de expediente sobre fabrica de una casa en Veracruz para la administración general de Real Hacienda y los planos respectivos a este proyecto.
28. Ibid., fols. 23v-34r.
29. BCM, ms. 5-2-4-3, Memoria sobre el reyno de Nueva España, Provincias Internas y Californias, Veracruz, 24 October 1815; Fireman, The Spanish Royal Corps, 186.
30. BNM, ms. 19266, Miguel Costanzó to Miguel José de Azanza, 6 January 1799.

Notes

31. Michael E. Thurman, The Naval Department of San Blas: New Spain's Bastion for Alta California and Nootka, 1767-1798 (Glendale, California: Arthur H. Clark Company, 1967), 183-186; Donald C. Cutter, Malaspina in California (San Francisco: John Howell Books, 1960), 80.

32. MN, Reyno de México III, ms. 335, Carta al Comercio de Mexico convidandole a un ensayo sobre el comercio de las pieles de nutrias, por Alejandro Malaspina.

33. AGN, Bandos, vol. 5, exp. 76, Bando de 23 de septiembre de 1763.

34. AGN, Historia, vol. 578, Copía original del memorial y proyecto de iluminación que tiene presentado Don Angel María Merelo, vecino de México, 17 May 1777.

35. AGN, Bandos, vol. 12, exp. 67, Bando de 6 de noviembre de 1783.

36. AGN, Bandos, vol. 14, exp. 51, Bando de 13 de febrero de 1787.

37. AGN, Bandos, vol. 15, exp. 56, fols. 158-161, Reglamenyo formado de ordén del Excmo. Señor Virrey Conde de Revilla Gigedo para el gobierno que ha de observarse en el alumbrado de las calles de México, dado el 6 de abril de 1790.

38. Revilla Gigedo, Instrucción reservada, articles 292-295.

Chapter 3

1. AGN, Virreyes, vol. 26, Carta No. 627 (reservada), Revillagigedo II to Gardoquí, 31 August 1793.

2. Doris M. Ladd, The Mexican Nobility at Independence, 1780-1826 (Austin: University of Texas Press, 1976), 25.

3. Enrique Florescano, Precios de maíz y crísis agrícola en México, 1708-1800 (México: El Colegio de México, 1969), 25.

4. Ladd, The Mexican Nobility, 37.

5. AGN, Bandos, vol. 18, Consejos utiles para socorrer a la necesidad en tiempo que escasean los comestibles, por Don José Antonio de Alzate y Ramírez.

6. Consumption within Mexico City in the middle of the seventeenth century was approximately 170,000 sheep, 12,000 cattle, 30,000 swine, 220,000 fanegas of maize, and 180,000 fanegas of flour as shown in Chester L. Guthrie, "Colonial Economy, Trade, Industry, and Labor in Seventeenth Century Mexico City," Revista de la historia de América 7 (December 1939), 104. See also Richard Boyer, "Mexico in the Seventeenth Century: Transition of a Colonial Society," Hispanic American Historical Review 57 (August 1977): 469-472 and Louisa S. Hoberman, "Merchants in Seventeenth-Century Mexico City: A Preliminary Portrait," Hispanic American Historical Review 57 (August 1977): 479-483.

Notes

7. A fanega is equal to approximately 1.5 English bushels. Most eighteenth century archival documents use this measurement when analyzing agricultural production and consumption. For a good historical study of the utilization of this measurement see Manuel Carrera Stampa, "The Evolution of Weights and Measures in New Spain," Hispanic American Historical Review 29 (February 1949): 2-24.

8. MN, Reyno de México III, ms. 335, Almonía de lo que se ha consumido en la capital de México, ano de 1788; MN, Pineda, Nueva España II, ms. 563, Noticía sucinta de la ciudad de Santiago de Querétaro, comprendida en la provincía y arzobispo de México, reino de Nueva España, en la América Septentrional. Extendida por el orden de las preguntas que contiene el interrogatoría del señor coronel Antonio Pineda primer teniente del regimiento de Reales Guardias Españolas de Infantería, 1791; Ladd, The Mexican Nobility, 39; O'Crouley, A Description, 30.

9. Brading, "La estructura de la producción agrícola en el Bajío de 1700 a 1850," Historia mexicana 23 (octubre-diciembre 1973): 200-205.

10. Charles H. Harris III, A Mexican Family Empire: The Latifundio of the Sanchez Navarros, 1765-1867 (Austin: University of Texas Press, 1975), 65-81; William B. Taylor, Landlord and Peasant in Colonial Oaxaca (Stanford: Stanford University Press, 1972), 195-202.

11. Brading, Miners and Merchants, 104-125; Wayne S. Osborn, "Indian Land Retention in Colonial Metztitlán," Hispanic American Historical Review 53 (May 1973): 226-235.

12. Brading, Miners and Merchants, 14.

13. Humboldt, Ensayo político, 250-251.

14. AHH, Consulado, leg. 917, exp. 2, Lista o noticía de las jurisdicciones o partidos de la comprensión de la provincía de Nueva Vizcaya, por Bernardo Bonavía, 1803.

15. BCM, ms. 5-2-1-7, Descripción de las provincias internas, 1797, por Juan Pagazaurtundúa; LC, Manuscript Division, Peter Force Papers, Series VIII-C, Item 5, Memorias sobre las provincias del norte de Nueva España.

16. Alexander von Humboldt, Political Essay on the Kingdom of New Spain, ed. Mary Maples Dunn (New York: Alfred A. Knopf, Inc., 1972), 101. For a more detailed analysis of Mexican agriculture see Susan L. Swan, "Climate, Crops, and Livestock: Some Aspects of Colonial Mexican Agriculture" (Ph.D. dissertation, Washington State University, 1977).

17. Humboldt, Ensayo político, 254-256.

18. Florescano, Precios de maíz, 111-146.

Notes

19. Humboldt, Political Essay, 104.
20. Humboldt, Ensayo político, 253-260.
21. AGN, Bandos, vol. 18, Consejos utiles para socorrer a la necesidad; Ladd, The Mexican Nobility, 38-39.
22. AHH, Consulado, leg. 917, exp. 1, Provincía de Guadalajara. Estado que demuestra los frutos y efectos de agricultura, industría y comercio que han producido los veinte y nueve partidos que comprende esta provincia en el año de 1803, por José Fernando de Abascal y Sousa; AHH, Consulado, leg. 917, exp. 5, Noticías estadísticas de la intendencía de Veracruz, 1803.
23. Humboldt, Ensayo político, 140-172; Hubert H. Bancroft, History of Mexico, 6 vols. (San Francisco: A.L. Bancroft Company, 1883-1888), 3: 617-618.
24. AGN, Reales Cédulas (Originales), vol. 107, exp. 229, 22 May 1776, Prohibí los generos finos conduce de Filipinas el navio que anualmente viene al puerto de Acapulco; AGN, Reales Cédulas (Originales), vol. 109, exp. 38, 19 October 1776, Que los tejidos que transporten a Filipinas no esten comprendidos en la prohibición.
25. AGI, México, leg. 2518, Expedientes del consulado y comercio (1817-1818), Memoría de Estatuto.
26. Ramón María Serrera Contreras, Cultivo y manufactura de lino y cañamo en Nueva España, 1777-1800 (Sevilla: Escuela de Estudios Hispano-Americanos, 1974), 93-118.
27. AGI, Indiferente, leg. 101, Representación que Don Miguel Gónzalez de Tejada hace al Rey Nuestro Señor sobre verificar su real mente en el admirable planteo y propagación de siembras de lino y cañamo en todas las ciudades, villas y pueblos de América.
28. Serrera Contreras, Cultivo, 196-213.
29. Revilla Gigedo, Instrucción reservada, articles 391-393.
30. AGI, Indiferente, leg. 1559, Instrucción para sembrar, cultivar y beneficiar el lino y cañamo en Nueva España, impresa de ordén del Excmo. Señor Virrey Marqués de Branciforte, 1796.
31. Humboldt, Ensayo político, 453.
32. AGN, Virreyes, vol. 26, Carta No. 627 (reservada), Revillagigedo II to Gardoquí, 31 August 1793.
33. Bancroft, History of Mexico, 3: 609-614.
34. AGN, Historía, vol. 72, exp. 24, Tablas geográficas políticas del reino de Nueva Espana, que manifiestan la superficie, población, agricultura, fabricas, comercio, minas, rentas y fuerza militar, 1804.
35. MN, Reyno de México III, ms. 335, Bebidas alcoholicas de México, 1790; AGN, Historia, vol. 72, exp. 24, Tablas geográficas políticas del reino de Nueva España; José Longiños Martínez, Journal of José Longiños Martínez: Notes and Observations of the Naturalist of the Botanical

Expedition in Old and New California, 1791-1792, ed. Lesley Byrd Simpson (San Francisco: John Howell Books, 1961), 1-17; Taylor, Drinking, Homicide, and Rebellion in Colonial Mexican Villages (Stanford: Stanford University Press, 1979), 30-33.

36. Bancroft Library (hereafter cited as BL), Mexican Manuscripts, vol. 9, fols. 33r-64v, Memoría sobre la naturaleza, cultivo y beneficio de la Grana-Cochina, 1777.

37. Brian R. Hamnett, Politics and Trade in Southern Mexico, 1750-1821 (Cambridge: Cambridge University Press, 1971), 56-57.

38. Hamnett, "Dye Production, Food Supply, and the Laboring Population of Oaxaca, 1750-1820," Hispanic American Historical Review 51 (February 1971): 60-61.

39. BL, Mexican Manuscripts, vol. 9, fols. 152-153, Memoría sobre la naturaleza.

40. AGN, Historia, vol, 72, exp. 24, Tablas geográficas políticas del reino de Nueva España; Hamnett, Trade, 170.

41. BCM, ms. 5-2-4-3, Memoria sobre el reyno de Nueva España. For a translation of this chronicle see John S. Leiby, Report to the King: Colonel Juan Camargo y Cavallero's Historical Account of New Spain, 1815 (New York: Peter Lang Publishing, Inc., 1984).

42. AGN, Tierras, vol. 1196, exp. 2, Con la Real Orden del 30 de enero de 1799, la Corona comisión la investigación de los buenos o malos efectos de las composiciones relativos a tierras realengas y baldias ségun la Real Instrucción de 1754.

43. AGN, Virreyes, vol. 26, Carta No. 627 (reservada), Revillagigedo II to Gardoquí, 31 August 1793.

44. AGI, México, leg. 2518, Expedientes del consulado y comercio (1817-1818), Memoría de Estatuto; BCM, ms. 5-2-4-3, Memoria sobre el reyno de Nueva España.

Chapter 4

1. William J. Callahan, "The Crown and the Promotion of Industry in Eighteenth-Century Spain" (Ph.D. dissertation, Harvard University, 1964), 119-167; AGN, Virreyes, vol. 26, Carta No. 627 (reservada), Revillagigedo II to Gardoquí, 31 August 1793.

2. Herr, The Eighteenth Century, 120-121.

3. AGI, México, leg. 1507, Instrucción reservada para el Marqués de Amarillas, electo virrey de Nueva España, dado el 30 de junio de 1755; Asunción Lavrin, "The Role of the Nunneries in the Economy of New Spain in the Eighteenth Century," Hispanic American Historical Review 46 (November 1966): 371-383.

4. Manuel Rivera Cambas, Los gobernantes de México, 6 vols. (México: Imprenta de J.M. Aguilar; reprint ed., México: Editorial Citlaltepetl, 1964), 3:33; José Antonio Calderón Quijano, "El banco de San Carlos y las comunidades de indios de Nueva España," Anuario de Estudios Americanos 18 (1962): 371-383.

5. Romulo Velasco Ceballos, ed., La administración de D. Frey Antonio María de Bucareli y Ursúa, 2 vols. (México: Publicaciones del Archivo General de la Nación, 1936), 2: 19-20.

6. Ibid., 266-269.

7. CECDNS, Carta No. 443, 27 March 1790, fols. 560-562, El virrey de N.E., conde de Revilla Gigedo, da cuenta con testimonio en que consta el privilegio que ha concedido a Don Manuel Ochoa para usar una nueva maquina de hilar sedas.

8. Revilla Gigedo, Instrucción reservada, articles 375-378.

9. CECDNS, Carta No. 56, 27 August 1790, fols. 59-61, El virrey de N.E., conde de Revilla Gigedo, dice las providencias que ha tomado para destemar en lo posible la desnudez e indecencía de las gentes del populacho de México.

10. Real ordenanza para el establecimiento e instrucción de intendentes de exército y provincía en el reino de Nueva España (Madrid: Imprenta de D. Joachín Ibarra, 1786), ordinance N. 11.

11. Ibid., ordinance N. 58.

12. Ibid., ordinance N. 160.

13. Luís Pérez Verdía, Historia particular del estado de Jalisco: desde los primeros tiempos de que hay noticía hasta nuestro días, 2 ed., 3 vols. (Guadalajara: Gráfica, 1952), 1: 456-457.

14. AGI, México, leg. 2518, Expedientes del consulado y comercio (1817-1818), Memoría de Estatuto.

15. AGI, México, leg. 1973, Titulo de Gobernador Intendente de Puebla de los Angeles a favor de don Manuel Flon, San Lorenzo, 19 October 1785; AGN, Historia, vol. 74, exp. 10, Noticía de fabricas, molinos, ingenios, lagunas, rios y puentes, 1794.

16. The names of the flour mills within Puebla were Santo Domingo, Agua Azul, Amatlán, Enmedio, Batán, La Teja, El Mayorazgo, Toledo, Rementería, Nuestra Señora de Guadalupe, San Francisco, San Antonio, El Cármen, and Huejottitlán.

17. AGN, Historia, vol. 74, exp. 10, fols. 407r-427v, Noticías de fabricas.

18. AGI, México, leg. 1973, Titulo de Gobernador Intendente de la provincía de Oaxaca a favor de don Antonio de Mora y Peysal.

19. AGN, Historia, vol. 74, exp. 10, fols. 427r-438v, Noticías de fabricas.

Notes

20. Ibid., fols. 438v-455r.
21. MN, Pineda, España II, ms. 563, Descripción de la Ciudad y Real de Minas de Guanajuato, 1788, por José Hernández Chico; AGN, Historia, vol. 74, exp. 10, fols. 438-446r, Noticías de fabricas.
22. British Museum (hereafter cited as BM), Add. MSS 577, fols. 147-149, Noticía breve sobre la industría textil de Querétaro, 1802.
23. Ibid., fol. 147.
24. BCM, ms. 5-2-4-3, Memoría sobre el reyno de Nueva España.
25. AGI, México, leg. 1809, fols. 14-17, Miguel Domínguez to Viceroy Félix Berenquer de Marquina, 17 November 1801.
26. Ibid., fols. 17-18.
27. Ibid., fols. 18-21.
28. AGI, México, leg. 2518, Expedientes del consulado y comercio (1817-1818), Memoría de Estatuto.
29. Humboldt, Ensayo político, 453.
30. AGI, México, leg. 2518, Expedientes del consulado y comercio (1817-1818), Memoría de Estatuto.
31. CECDNS, Carta No. 714, 28 February 1792, fols. 23v-26r, El virrey de N.E., expone la necesidad que hay que se remitan a Veracruz dos brigantines proporcionados para la condución a España de las maderas de mantages que existienen en aquel puerto y evitan de este suerte el deterioro a que estan expuestas.
32. AGI, México, leg. 2518, Expedientes del consulado y comercio (1817-1818), Memoría de Estatuto.
33. BCM, ms. 5-2-4-3, Memoria sobre el reyno de Nueva Espana.
34. AGN, Virreyes, vol. 28, Carta No. 468, Bucareli to Arriaga, 26 July 1772.
35. AGN, Historia, vol. 72, exp. 24, Tablas geográficas políticas del reino de Nueva España.
36. Humboldt, Ensayo político, 453.
37. Ibid., 454-455.
38. AGN, Historia, vol. 72, exp. 24, Tablas geográficas políticas del reino de Nueva España.
39. AGI, México, leg. 2518, Expedientes del consulado y comercio (1817-1818), Memoría de Estatuto.
40. Revilla Gigedo, Instrucción reservada, articles 1006-1007.
41. BCM, ms. 5-3-9-4, Varios pliegos sueltos que corresponden con diario de reconocimiento en Nueva España; BCM, ms. 5-3-9-14, Descripción de estas provincias de Culiacán, Sinaloa y Sonora, por Don Francisco Fersén; AGN, Virreyes, vol. 26, Carta No. 627 (reservada), Revillagigedo II to Gardoquí, 31 August 1793; MN, Pineda, Nueva España II, ms. 563, Descripción de la Ciudad y Real de Minas de Guanajuato.

Notes

42. MN, Reyno de México III, ms. 335, Noticías generales de las Reales Casas de Moneda y Apartado General de oro y plata de México por Señor Alejandro Malaspina, 1791; Humboldt, Ensayo político, 457-459.
43. AGI, México, leg. 2802, Rázon de las cantidades de oro y plata acuñada en la Real Casa de Moneda de México, 1794.
44. AGN, Historia, vol. 72, exp. 24, Tablas geográficas políticas del reino de Nueva España.
45. AGN, Virreyes, vol. 26, Carta No. 627 (reservada), Revillagigedo II to Gardoquí, 31 August 1793.
46. AGI, México, leg. 2518, Expedientes del consulado y comercio (1817-1818), Memoría de Estatuto.

Chapter 5

1. Haring, The Spanish Empire, 314-320.
2. AGI, Indiferente, leg. 2528, Real Cédula de 2 de abril de 1728; Manuel Carrera Stampa, "Las ferías novo-hispanas," Historia mexicana 7 (enero-marzo 1953): 320.
3. Carrera Stampa, "Las ferias," 321-327.
4. AGI, México, leg. 2984, Embarcaciones salidas para la América al nuevo proyecto de las islas de Barlovento.
5. AGN, Reales Cédulas (Originales), vol. 110, exp. 69, 24 January 1777, Al comprobarse la complicidad en ellos, al Alcalde de Tampico don Antonio Fernández Aguilar, se castigará severamente.
6. AGI, México, leg. 2986, Bando de 10 de octubre de 1772.
7. AGI, México, leg. 2987, Cortejo del valor que llevaron las flotas del Sr. Dn. Luís de Córdoba y la del Sr. Dn. Antonio de Ulloa y de los efectos vendidos y extraidos de la fería de Xalapa para lo anterior del reino al tiempo que una y otra dieron vela en Veracruz para su regreso a España, 1778.
8. Carrera Stampa, "Las ferías," 326-329; Jose Joaquín Real Díaz, "Las ferías de Jalapa," Anuario de Estudios Americanos 16 (1959): 269-280.
9. HNM, Gaceta de México, 10 January 1786, Tomo II, 5.
10. AGI, México, leg. 2505, Real decreto de 28 de febrero de 1789.
11. William L. Schurz, The Manila Galleon (New York: E.P. Dutton and Company, Inc., 1939), 361-387; Carrera Stampa, "Las ferías," 329-331.
12. MN,Filipinas III, ms. 313, Real ordén de S.M. para el establecimiento de un cuerpo de comerciantes en la ciudad de Manila con incerción del Reglamento de 8 de abril de 1734 sobre el methodo que se trade obserban enla práctica del comercio de las Islas Philipin.[s] con el reyno de Nueva España.

13. MN, Filipinas III, ms. 313, Real cédula de erección de la Compañía de Filipinas de 10 de marzo de 1785.

14. CECDNS, Carta No. 352, 26 February 1790, fols. 250-269r, El virrey de N.E., dice haver concedido al comercio de Filipinas el embarco de 500,000 pesos de sobrantes de la precedente expedientes apoyas con robunos motivo la providencía y pide ampliación para esta clase de retornos.

15. BCM, ms. 5-2-4-3, Memoría sobre el reyno de Nueva España.

16. Carrera Stampa, "Las ferías," 334-336.

17. Richard L. Garner, "Zacatecas, 1750-1821: The Study of a Late Colonial Mexican City" (Ph.D. dissertation, University of Michigan, 1970), 279.

18. AGN, Virreyes, vol. 26, Carta No. 627 (reservada), Revillagigedo II to Gardoquí, 31 August 1793.

19. Humboldt, Ensayo político, 579; Brading, "Government and Elite in Late Colonial Mexico," Hispanic American Historical Review 53 (August 1973): 393. The term comerciante probably included the cajeros (apprentices) and the tratantes (tradesmen).

20. Brading, Miners and Merchants, 104-115.

21. Ladd, The Mexican Nobility, 35.

22. CECDNS, Carta No. 706, 31 January 1792, fols. 14v-18r, El virrey de N.E., da cuenta con testimonio de las providencías que ha tomado en conseguirla de la real ordenes de 29 de septiembre de 1790 y 19 maio de 1791 sobre contrata de maderas para montages y pronta remisión a España de la que existen en aquello almacenes.

23. Edith B. Couturier, "Hacienda de Hueyapan: The History of a Mexican Social and Economic Institution, 1550-1940" (Ph.D. dissertation, Columbia University, 1965), 63-64.

24. BCM, ms. 5-2-4-3, Memoría sobre el reyno de Nueva España.

25. Brading, Miners and Merchants, 102.

26. Riley, "The Management," 184-187.

27. Christiana Renate Moreno, Kaufmannschaft und Handelskapitalismus in der Stadt Mexiko, 1759-1778 (Bonn: Rheinische Friedrich-Wilhelms-Universität, 1978), 72-142.

28. AGN, Virreyes, vol. 26, Carta No. 627 (reservada), Revillagigedo II to Gardoquí, 31 August 1793.

29. AGI, México, leg. 2506, Expedientes del consulado y comercio, Real cédula de 17 de enero de 1795.

30. AGI, Guadalajara, leg. 526, Expedientes sobre la ereccion y cuentas del consulado, Real cédula de 8 de junio de 1795.

31. AGI, México, leg. 2506, articles 22-30.

32. AGI, México, leg. 1818, Expedientes inventariados (1808): Expediente sobre la extinción de los consulados de Veracruz y Guadalajara, Branciforte to Godoy, 26 September 1796.

Notes

33. James M. Manfredini, "The Political Role of the Count of Revillagigedo, Viceroy of New Spain, 1789-1794" (Ph.D. dissertation, University of Texas, Austin, 1949), 64-68.

34. AGN, Bandos, vol. 16, exp. 39, Reglamento para los mercados de México, 1791.

35. Ibid., 98-99.

36. Ibid., 99-100.

37. Revilla Gigedo, Instrucción reservada, articles 300-303.

38. Azanza, Instrucción reservada, 64-66.

39. CECDNS, Carta No. 312, 26 February 1790, fols. 160-161, El virrey de N.E., contesta real orden sobre la Compañía Marítima que se estableció en España.

40. MN, Papeles Varios IV, ms. 317, Extracto de lo principal que contiene un papel presentado al Seren.mo Señor Principe Generalisimo Almirante en 21 de Julio de 1807 sobre nuestro comercio marítimo ségun su actual estado, por Vicente Basadre. Another copy of this pertinent document can found in AGI, Indiferente General, leg. 2439.

41. In Mexico customhouses were located in the following urban centers: Mexico City, Acapulco, Puebla, Oaxaca, Tlaxcala, Querétaro, Tepeaca, Tabasco, Toluca, Celaya, Guanajuato, León, Cuernavaca, Zacatecas, Guadalajara, Córdoba, Orizaba, Valladolid, San Miguel el Grande, Tampico, San Luís Potosí, Durango, Zamora, Jalapa, Veracruz, Chihuahua, Bolaños, Tehuantepec, Zacatlán, Apam, Tlalpujuhua, Pachuca, and Fresnillo.

42. MN, Reyno de México III, ms. 335, Estado que manifiesta por aduanas los resguardos que mantiene la renta de alcabalas y pulques de este reino de Nueva España y los sueldos que seles pagan por la misma renta; AGI, México, leg. 1507, Instrucción reservada para el Marqués de Amarillas electo virrey de Nueva España, dado el 30 de junio de 1755.

43. MN, Reyno de México III, ms. 335, Rázon de los dineros que exigen a todos los efectos asi nacionales y extrangeros, que se introducen en este puerto de los de Europa, como tambien los que satisfacen los procedentes de otros puertos de América igualmente los que adeuden su extracción todos los efectos.

44. Ibid.

45. MN, Reyno de México III, ms. 335, La exportación del puerto de Veracruz en 1802, 1803 y 1804.

46. AGN, Historia, vol. 72, exp. 24, Tablas geográficas políticas del reino de Nueva España; MN, Reyno de México III, ms. 335, La exportación del puerto de Veracruz.

Notes

47. BCM, ms. 5-2-4-3, Memoría sobre el reyno de Nueva España.

48. MN, Reyno de Mexico III, ms. 335, La exportación del puerto de Veracruz; BCM, ms. 5-2-4-3, Memoría sobre el reyno de Nueva España.

Chapter 6

1. For the economic and political decline in Spain during the late seventeenth century see John H. Elliot, Imperial Spain, 1469-1716 (New York: St. Martin's Press, 1963), 368-376 and John Lynch, Spain Under the Hapsburgs, 2 vols. (New York: Oxford University Press, 1964-1969), 2: 238-264.

2. A recent monograph which portrays the early Bourbon attempts at economic reform is Geoffrey J. Walker, Spanish Politics and Imperial Trade, 1700-1789 (Bloomington: Indiana University Press, 1979), 1-82.

3. Campillo's treatise was a remarkable work which spurred on the Bourbon monarchs to initiate economic reforms see Chapter 1 of the present work. Campillo, Nuevo sistema, 29-74.

4. John H. Parry, The Sale of Public Office in the Spanish Indies Under the Hapsburgs (Berkeley: University of California Press, 1953), 53-82.

5. Lynch, Spanish Colonial Administration, 1782-1810: The Intendant System in the Viceroyalty of the Rio de la Plata (London: Clarendon Press, 1958), 168-202.

6. Zabala y Lera, España bajo los Borbones, 54-68.

7. Priestley, José de Gálvez, 2-28.

8. Ibid.

9. Biblioteca del Palacio Real (hereafter cited as BPR), MSS 2816, Miscelanía de Ayala, 278, fols. 129-130.

10. Jose de Galvez, Informe general...al excelentísimo señor virrey d. frey Antonio Bucareli y Ursúa (México, 1867), 3.

11. AGI, Indiferente General, leg. 1713, José de Gálvez to Marqués de Croix, 15 January 1768.

12. Ibid.

13. Ibid.

14. Brading, Miners and Merchants, 56-62.

15. Lynch, Spanish Colonial Administration, 1-54.

16. AGI, México, leg. 1510, Royal Orders of Charles III, 14 August 1779. The viceroy was placed in overall charge of the Royal Exchequer while Cossío was placed immediately below the viceroy, although with special exchequer powers.

17. BCM, ms. 5-2-4-3, Memoría sobre el reyno de Nueva España. See also Leiby, Report to the King, 1-26.

Notes

18. AGI, México, leg. 1391, Moraga to Gálvez, 28 September 1782; AGI, México, leg. 1878, Cossío to Valdés, 20 October 1787.

19. Brading, Miners and Merchants, 63.

20. Luís Navarro García, Intendencias de Indias (Sevilla: Escuela de Estudios Hispano-Americanos, 1959), 60-61.

21. CECDNS, Dictamen que en cumplimiento de Reales Ordenes de S.M. produce el Virrey de Nueva España, Conde de Revillagigedo, sobre la precisión de adiccionar la Ordenanza de Yntendentes expedida en 4 de diciembre de 1786.

22. Ibid.

23. Navarro García, Intendencias, 114-116.

24. Ibid.

25. AGI, México, leg. 1973, Mangiño to Gálvez, 15 July 1787.

26. AGI, México, leg. 1532, Revillagigedo II to Lerena, 26 September 1790.

27. Biblioteca Nacional de México (hereafter cited as BMEX), MSS 432 (1391), fol. 60.

28. Revilla Gigedo, Instrucción reservada, 115.

29. AGN, Virreyes, vol. 26, Carta No. 627 (reservada), Revillagigedo II to Gardoquí, 31 August 1793.

30. AGI, México, leg. 1579, Intendant Reports, 1792. All of the intendants in 1791 were instructed to compile an economic report and dispatch it to Viceroy Revillagigedo. Most of these reports can be found in this particular legajo although some of them are missing. Revillagigedo clearly understood the increasing role of the colonial bureaucracy in promoting economic development.

31. Ibid. Flon was the intendant of Puebla; Mora that of Oaxaca; Díaz that of Valladolid; Diaz del Salcedo that of San Luís Potosí; Valdés that of Zacatecas; Riaño that of Guanajuato; and Abascal that of the intendancy of Guadalajara. Those missing are from the intendants of Veracruz, Yucatán, Nueva Vizcaya, and Sonora.

32. AGN, Historia, vol. 74, exp. 10, fols. 407r-455r, Noticías de fabricas. This manuscript provides the intendant reports of 1794. Another copy of this document is located in BL, Mexican Manuscripts, vol. 9.

33. John E. Kicza, Colonial Entrepreneurs: Families and Business in Bourbon Mexico City (Albuquerque: University of New Mexico Press, 1983), 160-161; Richard B. Lindley, Haciendas and Economic Development: Guadalajara, Mexico at Independence (Austin: University of Texas Press, 1983), 14-28 and Revilla Gigedo, Instrucción reservada, 128-130. Kicza is currently working on another book which will contain a section on the bureaucrats in Bourbon Mexico City.

34. CECDNS, Dictamen...1790.

35. Revillagigedo has the reputation in Mexican history of being an enlightened bureaucrat. However, more importantly he supported a strong central government to the detriment of the colonial elites. He found creole society in late Bourbon Mexico distasteful to him. Their affluence amid the poverty of New Spain made him even more scornful of them. See AGN, Virreyes, vol. 26, Carta No. 627 (reservada), Revillagigedo II to Gardoquí, 31 August 1793. Controversy, however, exists as to the benefits achieved under the Bourbon reforms and especially from the inclusion of the Mexican colony in the system of comercio libre. See Stanley J. Stein, "Bureaucracy and Business in the Spanish Empire, 1759-1804: Failure of a Bourbon Reform in Mexico and Peru," Hispanic American Historical Review 61 (February 1981): 2-28.

36. Ibid. See also Leiby, Report to the King, 1-26 and Revilla Gigedo, Instrucción reservada, 1-28.

37. AGN, Historia, vol. 72, exp. 24, Tablas geográficas políticas del reino de Nueva España; Leiby, Report to the King, 30-33.

Chapter 7

1. Magali Sarfatti, Spanish Bureaucratic-Patrimonialism in America (Berkeley and Los Angeles: Institute of International Studies, 1966), 1-54. See also John J. TePaske and Herbert S. Klein, "The Seventeenth-Century Crisis in New Spain: Myth and Reality?" Past and Present 90 (1981): 116-135. TePaske and Klein refute the "crisis" theory by analyzing the income of the Royal treasuries in Mexico City and Lima between 1580 and 1820. Both treasuries showed marked increases during the late colonial epoch.

2. AGN, Virreyes, vol. 26, Carta No. 627 (reservada), Revillagigedo II to Gardoquí, 31 August 1793; Navarro García, Intendencias, 28-35. Revillagigedo came into office in 1789 and throughout his viceregency advocated fiscal reform. Only if revenues continued to increase could New Spain's bureaucracy and government expand.

3. For an analysis of the revival of mining see Brading, "Mexican Silver-Mining in the Eighteenth Century: The Revival of Zacatecas," Hispanic American Historical Review 50 (November 1970): 665-681.

4. Gálvez, Informe, 3-43. A copy of this informe can be found in MN, Reyno de México III, ms. 335. Another copy is located in the Real Academía de la Historía, Madrid. I was not able to use this latter, however, there exists little difference among the texts.

Notes

5. Brading, Miners and Merchants, 63-74.
6. AGN, Historia, vol. 72, exp. 24, Tablas geográficas políticas del reino de Nueva España.
7. MN, Reyno de México III, ms. 335, Estado general de los créditos y Deudas interiores, que tenían las tesorerias Reales de Nueva España en fin del año de 1789.
8. Ibid., Estado que manifiesta por Aduanas los Resguardos.
9. BCM, ms. 2-3-4-2 and 2-3-4-4, Ingenieros en México y Filipinas.
10. MN, Reyno de México III, ms. 335, Estado general de los créditos y Deudas interiores.
11. Ibid. See also Gálvez, Informe, 93.
12. AGN, Virreyes, vol. 26, Carta No. 627 (reservada), Revillagigedo II to Gardoquí, 31 August 1793.
13. MN, Reyno de México III, ms. 335, Estado general de los créditos y Deudas interiores.
14. Ibid.
15. Ibid. The records located in the Museo Naval, Madrid, Spain are rather detailed and accurate. I have compared them to similar manuscripts held by the Archivo General de la Nación.
16. CECDNS, Carta No. 17, 27 July 1790, fols. 21r-23r, Remite testimonio de expediente sobre fabrica de una casa en Veracruz para la administración general de Real Hacienda y los planos respectivos a este proyecto. The complete story concerning the customhouse "controversy" is found in Chapter 2 of this present study.
17. MN, Reyno de México III, ms. 335, Estado que manifiesta los empleados que mantiene el Ramo de Polvora de este Reino de Nueva España y sueldos que se les pagan por el mismo ramo.
18. AGN, Historia, vol. 72, exp. 24, Tablas geográficas políticas del reino de Nueva España; Humboldt, Ensayo político, 543-548.
19. MN, Reyno de México III, ms. 335, Ramo de Polvora. For an explanation of the social structure in Bourbon Mexico see Lyle N. McAlister, "Social Structure and Social Change in New Spain," Hispanic American Historical Review 43 (August 1963): 349-370.
20. MN, Reyno de México III, ms. 335, Estado que manifiesta los empleados que mantiene la Renta de Naipes de este Reino de Nueva España y sueldos que se les pagan por la misma renta.
21. AGN, Historia, vol. 72, exp. 24, Tablas geográficas políticas del reino de Nueva España.
22. MN, Reyno de México III, ms. 335, Renta de Naipes.
23. Real ordenanza para el establecimiento e instrucción de intendentes, ordinances N. 12-23.

Notes

24. BL, Mexican Manuscripts, vol. 9, Notiсía geográfica del Reino de Nueva España y estado de su población, agricultura, artes y comercio, 1794.

25. Revilla Gigedo, Instrucción reservada, articles 740-741; MN, Reyno de México III, ms. 335, Estado General de los valores y distribución que han tenido los Ramos Comunes, y Particular de la Real Hacienda en las tesorerías de N.E. el año de 1790.

26. MN, Reyno de México III, ms. 335, Report on the Royal Mint, 1791, Francisco Fernández Córdoba.

27. Ibid.

28. Priestley, José de Gálvez, 1-28 and Galvez, Informe, 1-44.

29. MN, Reyno de México III, ms. 335, Estado que manifiesta por Aduanas.

30. AGN, Virreyes, vol. 26, Carta No. 627 (reservada), Revillagigedo II to Gardoquí, 31 August 1793; Revilla Gigedo, Instrucción reservada, articles 739-756.

Chapter 8

1. Manfredini, "Count of Revillagigedo," 24-44; Revilla Gigedo, Instruccion reservada, articles 829-835.

2. Brading, Miners and Merchants, 56-63; Manfredini, "Count of Revillagigedo," 1-24.

3. Ibid.

4. CECDNS, Dictamen que en cumplimiento de Reales Ordenes; MN, Reyno de México III, ms. 335, Estado general de los créditos y Deudas.

5. Revilla Gigedo, Instrucción reservada, articles 739-743.

6. AGN, Virreyes, vol. 26, Carta No. 627 (reservada), Revillagigedo II to Gardoquí, 31 August 1793. For the exact tithe estimates see Chapter 3.

7. AGN, Virreyes, vol. 25, Carta No. 405 (reservada), Revillagigedo II to Gardoquí, 15 March 1792. For the impact of comercio libre on Spain see John R. Fisher, "Imperial 'Free Trade' and the Hispanic Economy, 1778-1796," Journal of Latin American Studies 13 (1981): 21-56. Historians still disagree over the merits of comercio libre in revitalizing the Spanish American economy. The leading historians who question this interpretation are Stanley J. Stein and James Lockhart. See also James Lockhart and Stuart B. Schwartz, Early Latin America: A History of Colonial Spanish America and Brazil (Cambridge: Cambridge University Press, 1983), 361-366.

8. MN, Reyno de México III, ms. 335, La exportación del puerto de Veracruz; BL, Mexican Manuscripts, vol. 9, Noticía geográfica. See also Leiby, Report to the King, 117-119.

Notes

9. AGN, Virreyes, vol. 23, Carta No. 356 (reservada), Revillagigedo II to Valdés, 3 March 1791; AGN, Virreyes, vol. 25, Carta No. 405 (reservada), Revillagigedo II to Gardoquí, 15 March 1792; Revilla Gigedo, Instrucción reservada, articles 1322-1328.

10. Fernand Braudel, The Wheels of Commerce: Civilization and Capitalism, 15th-18th Century (New York: Harper and Row, Inc., 1982), 284-343.

11. AGN, Historia, vol. 72, exp. 24, Tablas geográficas políticas del reino de Nueva España; BL, Mexican Manuscripts, vol. 9, Noticía geográfica; Leiby, Report to the King, 112-130; Humboldt, Ensayo político, 50, 504.

12. AGN, Virreyes, vol. 25, Carta No. 258 (reservada), Revillagigedo II to Valdés, 31 November 1791; BL, Mexican Manuscripts, vol. 9, Noticía geográfica.

13. BCM, ms. 2-3-4-2 and 2-3-4-4, Ingenieros en México y Filipinas. For specific details concerning the activities of the Royal Corps of Engineers during the Revillagigedo see Miguel del Corral's biographical sketch.

14. MN, Reyno de México III, ms. 335, Estado que manifiesta por Aduanas.

15. BCM, ms. 2-3-4-3 and 2-3-4-4, Ingenieros en México y Filipinas; Revilla Gigedo, Instrucción reservada, articles 173-185.

16. Revilla Gigedo, Instrucción reservada, articles 186-196.

17. Humboldt, Ensayo político, 462, 463, 482, 564.

18. AGI, México, leg. 27, Relación de Enrico Martínez, 20 July 1608; BNM, ms. 3534, Relación sucinta de las Ynundaciones generales que han ocurido sobre la Ciudad de México desde su fundación, 1777. See also Hoberman, "Bureaucracy and Disaster: Mexico City and the Flood of 1629," Journal of Latin American Studies 6 (November 1974): 211-230.

19. BCM, ms. 2-3-4-4, Ingenieros en México y Filipinas. Revillagigedo's predecessor was Manuel Antonio Valdés.

20. BNM, ms. 3534, Revillagigedo II to Consulado(José de Cevallos?), 24 July 1790.

21. Ibid.; Revilla Gigedo, Instrucción reservada, articles 255-272.

22. BL, Mexican Manuscripts, vol. 9, Extracto de los treinta tomos del Libro de la Rázon general de Real Hacienda de Nueva España, 1793, por Don Carlos de Urrutía.

23. MN, Reyno de México III, ms. 335, Estado general de los créditos y Deudas interiores.

24. AGN, Virreyes, vol. 26, Carta No. 627 (reservada), Revillagigedo II to Gardoquí, 31 August 1793.

25. Ibid.

26. AGI, México, leg. 1818, Carta No. 336 (reservada), Marqués de Branciforte to Godoy, 26 September 1796; AGI, México, leg. 1818, Branciforte to Godoy, 31 March 1798.
27. AGN, Virreyes, vol. 26, Carta No. 627 (reservada), Revillagigedo II to Gardoquí, 31 August 1793.
28. Ibid.
29. BL, Mexican Manuscripts, vol. 9, Idea Sucinta de Metalurgía, 1792, por Don José Antonio Ribera Sánchez.
30. AGI, México, leg. 1579, Intendant Reports (1792-1794). These reports are rather extensive and number into several hundred pages.
31. Revilla Gigedo, _Instrucción reservada_, articles 308-406, 829-845.
32. AGN, Virreyes, vol. 26, Carta No. 627 (reservada), Revillagigedo II to Gardoquí, 31 August 1793.
33. Humboldt, _Ensayo político_, 504.

Chapter 9

1. AGN, Historia, vol. 72, exp. 24, Tablas geográficas políticas del reino de Nueva España; Zabala y Lera, _Espana bajo los Borbones_, 138-139.
2. Linda Jo Arnold, "Bureaucracy and Bureaucrats in Mexico City: 1742-1835" (Ph.D. dissertation, University of Texas, Austin, 1982), 1-35. A recent monograph which explains thoroughly the politics involved in Spain's loss of Spanish America is Timothy E. Anna, _Spain and the Loss of America_ (Lincoln: University of Nebraska Press, 1983).
3. RAH, Coleccion Muñoz, Ms 49; Bitar Letayf, _Economistas españoles_, 97-109. For a total description of the political and economic conditions in Spain during the late eighteenth century see Herr, _The Eighteenth Century Revolution_, 1-68.
4. RAH, Coleccion Muñoz, Ms 49. Copies of Uztariz's works can also be found in the Palacio del Oriente in Madrid, Spain.
5. Ibid.
6. Zabala y Lera, _España bajo los Borbones_, 142-143.
7. José Campillo y Cossío, _Nuevo sistema de gobierno económico para la América_ (Madrid: Imprenta de J. Ibarra, 1789); RAH, Coleccion Muñoz, Ms 49.
8. Ward, _Proyecto económico_, 13-56; RAH, Coleccion Munoz, Ms 49.
9. Flórez Estrada, _Examen imparcial de las disensiones de la América_, 1-24.
10. Ibid., 68-93.
11. Colin M. MacLachlan and Jaime E. Rodríguez O., _The Forging of the Cosmic Race: A Reinterpretation of Colonial Mexico_ (Berkeley: University of California Press, 1980), 288-289.

Notes

12. BL, Mexican Manuscripts, vol. 9, Memoría sobre la naturaleza.

13. Ibid.

14. AGN, Bandos, vol. 18, Consejos utiles para socorrer.

15. AGN, Virreyes, vol. 26, Carta No. 627 (reservada), Revillagigedo II to Gardoquí, 31 August 1793.

16. Ibid.

17. AGI, México, leg. 1818, Carta No. 336 (reservada), Branciforte to Godoy, 26 September 1796; AGI, México, leg. 1818, Branciforte to Godoy, 31 March 1798.

18. MacLachlan and Rodríguez O., Cosmic Race, 296-298; Nettie L. Benson, ed., Mexico and the Spanish Cortes, 1810-1822 (Austin: University of Texas Press, 1966), 1-10. A new book which examines the Hispanic economy and the increasing influence of Madrid is David R. Ringrose, Madrid and the Spanish Economy, 1560-1850 (Berkeley: University of California Press, 1983).

19. Ladd, The Mexican Nobility, 123-126. For the impact of taxes on Spain's overseas trade see Javier Esteban Cuenca, "Statistics of Spain's Colonial Trade, 1792-1820: Consular Duties, Cargo Inventories, and Balances of Trade," Hispanic American Historical Review 61 (August 1981): 381-428. For Veracruz's trade balances during this same period see Leiby, Report to the King, 117-119.

20. Arnold J. Bauer, "The Church in the Economy of Spanish America: Censos and Depósitos in the Eighteenth and Nineteenth Centuries," Hispanic American Historical Review 63 (November 1983): 717, 729-731. See also Ladd, The Mexican Nobility, 123-128.

21. Bancroft, History of Mexico, 4: 22-29; AGN, Historia, vol. 72, exp. 24, Tablas geográficas políticas del reino de Nueva España.

22. The Gaceta de México was published between 1784 and 1804. Thereafter the Diario de México became the official newspaper or pamphlet of the viceroyalty. See HNM, 1784-1804. I have also located a few copies of this newspaper in BCM, ms. 5-2-3-11, Gacetas de México.

23. Ladd, The Mexican Nobility, 148-149. See also Manuel Lucena Salmoral, "La Memoria de Basadre de 1818 sobre comercio y contrabando en el Caribe," Jahrbuch für Geschichte von Staat, Wirtschaft und Gesellschaft Lateinamerikas 18 (1982): 223-237.

24. MN, Papeles Varios IV, ms. 317, Extracto de lo principal; MN, Papeles Varios IV, ms. 317, Noticia del Comercio que han hecho los buques neutrales en el Puerto de Veracruz desde 26 de Septiembre de 1805 hasta fin de Abril de 1807. See also Leiby, Report to the King, 117-119.

25. AHH, Consulado, leg. 1040, exp. 14, Reflexiones. In 1793 Viceroy wrote a much detailed analysis of the

benefits achieved under comercio libre. See also AGN, Virreyes, vol. 26, Carta No. 627 (reservada), 31 August 1793.

26. AGI, México, leg. 2518, Expedientes del consulado y comercio (1817-1818), Memoría de Estatuto.

27. The basic accounts of the Hidalgo and Morelos Revolts are Hugh M. Hamill, The Hidalgo Revolt: Prelude to Mexican Independence (Gainesville: University of Florida Press, 1966) and Wilbert H. Timmons, Morelos of Mexico: Priest, Soldier, Statesman (El Paso: Texas Western Press, 1963).

28. Ibid.

29. BCM, ms. 5-2-4-3, Memoría sobre el reyno de Nueva España.

30. Anna, The Fall of the Royal Government in Mexico City (Lincoln: University of Nebraska Press, 1978), 120-149; MacLachlan and Rodríguez O., Cosmic Race, 328-329.

31. LC, H.P. Kraus Collection, Collection of Documents Relating to Spanish America, 1500-1819 (hereafter cited as HKC), Apodaca to Ministro de Guerra, 31 July 1819; Ibid., 31 August 1819; Ibid., 30 September 1819; Ibid., 31 October 1819; Ibid., 30 November 1819; Ibid., 31 December 1819.

32. In essence, the actions of Ferdinand VII and the Spanish Cortes caused the schism within Mexican society. Eventually the Mexican elites realized that moderate autonomy was no longer possible given the extent of anti-colonial attitudes within Spain. See Anna, Spain and the Loss of America, 64, 84, 219, 245.

33. By 1821 the colonial ethos had been destroyed largely by the events in Spain and Mexico. The Mexican noibility even helped Iturbide in reaching his objective. See Ladd, The Mexican Nobility, 124-125 and Bancroft, History of Mexico, 4: 730-733.

34. Barbier, "Peninsular Finance and Colonial Trade: The Dilemma of Charles IV's Spain," Journal of Latin American Studies 12 (May 1980): 21-37.

35. Anna, "Spain and the Breakdown of the Imperial Ethos: The Problem of Equality," Hispanic American Historical Review 62 (May 1982): 254-272.

Chapter 10

1. Several general histories of Mexico are quite good and readable but one in particular has come to the forefront in the last few years. See Michael C. Meyer and William L. Sherman, The Course of Mexican History, 2 ed. (New York: Oxford University Press, 1983). For the period between 1821 and 1910 see chapters 5,6, and 7.

Notes

2. Two books explain in detail the life and times of Francisco Madero. See Charles C. Cumberland, Mexican Revolution: Genesis Under Madero (Austin: University of Texas Press, 1952) and Stanley R. Ross, Francisco I. Madero: Apostle of Mexican Democracy (New York: Columbia University Press, 1955). The latter work is especially relevant because of its analysis of Madero's political thought.

3. Roderic Camp, a political scientist, has developed some socio-political studies which help to explain the development of the patrimonial state in modern Mexico. See Roderic A. Camp, Mexico's Leaders: Their Education and Recruitment (Tucson: University of Arizona Press, 1980) and Peter H. Smith, Labyrinths of Power: Political Recruitment in Twentieth-Century Mexico (Princeton: Princeton University Press, 1979).

4. For the population shifts since 1910 see James W. Wilkie, The Mexican Revolution: Federal Expenditure and Social Change Since 1910 (Berkeley: University of California Press, 1967). See especially Wilkie's appendices.

5. Ibid.

6. The best overall study in English about Carranza and the Constitutionalists remains Cumberland, Mexican Revolution: The Constitutionalist Years (Austin: University of Texas Press, 1972). A book which explains the political maneuvering during the drafting of the 1917 Constitution is E.V. Niemeyer, Revolution at Queretaro: The Mexican Constitutional Convention of 1916-1917 (Austin: University of Texas Press, 1974).

7. A concise study of educational reform in twentieth-century Mexico is Rámon Eduardo Ruíz, Mexico: The Challenge of Poverty and Illiteracy (San Marino: Huntington Library, 1963).

8. An uneven yet important study of Cardenas is William C. Townsend, Lázaro Cárdenas: Mexican Democrat (Ann Arbor: George Wahr Publishing Co., 1952). This particular work pays close attention to Cárdenas' agrarian reforms. For oil expropriation see Merril Rippy, "The Economic Repercussions of Expropriation: Case Study, Mexico," Inter-American Economic Affairs 5 (1951): 52-70.

9. José Luís Reyna, "Redefining the Authoritarian Regime," in Authoritarianism in Mexico (Philadelphia: Institute for the Study of Human Issues, 1977), 24-53 and Kenneth F. Johnson, Mexican Democracy: A Critical View (New York: Praeger Publishers, 1978), 14-18.

10. An excellent yet controversial book on political development in the underdeveloped world is Samuel P. Huntington, Political Order in Changing Societies (New Haven: Yale University Press, 1970).

11. For contemporary Mexico see Martin Needleman, "Who Rules Mexico? A Critique of Some Current Views on the Mexican Political Process," Journal of Politics 31 (November 1969): 1011-1034. For an analysis of Spanish institutions see Frank J. Moreno, "The Spanish Colonial System: A Functional Approach," Western Historical Quarterly 20 (1967): 308-320.
12. Ibid.
13. Reyna, "Redefining," 155.
14. David Felix, "Income Inequality in Mexico," Current History 72 (March 1977): 111-114; Brading, "Los españoles en México hacía 1792," Historia mexicana 21 (julio-septiembre 1973): 126-144.
15. Ibid.
16. Camp, Mexico's Leaders, 208-253; Brading, "Government and Elite," 389-414.
17. Ibid. See also Linda Jo Arnold, "Bureaucracy and Bureaucrats," 1-56.
18. Bo Anderson and James Cockcraft," Control and Cooptation in Mexican Politics," International Journal of Comparative Sociology 7 (March 1966): 12.
19. MacLachlan and Rodríguez O., Cosmic Race, 268-270; Anna, "The Last Viceroys of New Spain and Peru: An Appraisal," American Historical Review 81 (February 1976): 38-65.
20. Ibid., 283-285, 296.
21. Revilla Gigedo, Instrucción reservada, articles 1-24; BCM, ms. 2-3-4-2 and 2-3-4-4, Ingenieros en México y Filipinas.
22. MacLachlan and Rodríguez O., Cosmic Race, 270-274.
23. Luís A. López Escutía, "Ideología de las instituciones políticas mexicanas," Pensamiento político 66 (octubre 1974): 165-166; Miguel A. Gónzalez Rodríguez, "La politización: el desarrollo político," Pensamiento político 35 (marzo 1972): 357-368.
24. Ibid.
25. See Christon I. Archer, The Army in Bourbon Mexico, 1760-1810 (Albuquerque: University of New Mexico Press, 1977), 1-56 and Archer, "The Army of New Spain and the Wars of Independence," Hispanic American Historical Review 61 (November 1981): 705-714.
26. Paul J. Vanderwood, "Mexico's Rurales: Image of a Society in Transition," Hispanic American Historical Review 61 (February 1981): 52-83 and Vanderwood, Disorder and Progress: Bandits, Police, and Mexican Development (Lincoln: University of Nebraska Press, 1981).
27. Meyer and Sherman, The Course of Mexican History, 569-592. This part of the book describes the politics and events of the 1920s.

MAPS

Map 1 New Spain's Political Divisions (1815) Source: David Brading, Miners and Merchants in Bourbon Mexico, 1763-1810 (Cambridge: Cambridge University Press, 1971), 370. Reprinted by Permission of Cambridge University Press.

Map 2 Important Commercial Centers in Late Colonial Mexico

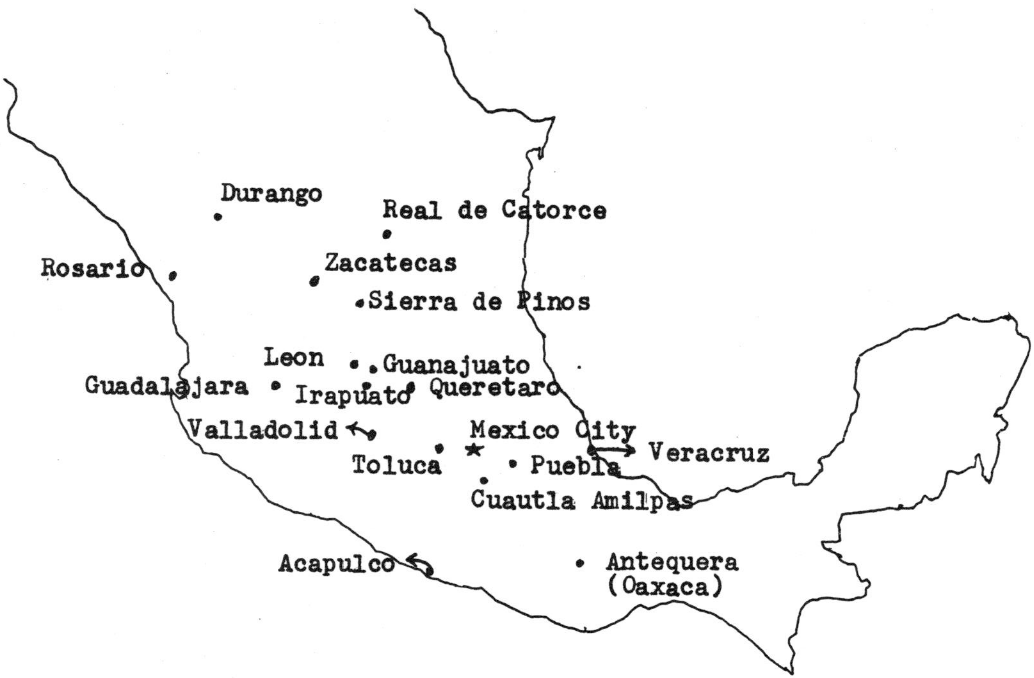

BIBLIOGRAPHY

A. PRIMARY SOURCES

SPAIN

Archivo General de las Indias, Sevilla

Audiencia de México, legajos 27, 1391, 1505, 1510, 1532, 1579, 1809, 1818, 1878, 1973, 2502, 2506, 2518, 2986, 2987

Audiencia de Guadalajara, legajos 301, 526

Indiferente General, legajos 432, 542, 1713, 1885, 2439

Indiferente de Nueva España, legajos 101, 1559, 2528

Archivo Histórico Nacional, Madrid

Diversos, legajo 472

Biblioteca Central Militar, Madrid

Manuscripts 2-3-4-2, 2-3-4-3, 2-3-4-4, 2-3-4-7, 5-2-1-7, 5-2-3-11, 5-2-4-3, 5-3-9-4, 5-3-9-5, 5-3-9-14

Biblioteca del Palacio Real, Madrid

MSS 2816, Miscelania de Ayala (278)

Biblioteca Nacional de Madrid, Madrid

Manuscripts 477, 3534, 19266

Museo Naval, Madrid

Reyno de México III, Manuscript 335

Papeles Varios IV, Manuscript 317

Filipinas III, Manuscript 313

Pineda, Nueva España II, Manuscript 563

Real Academía de la Historía, Madrid

Coleccion de Juan Bautista Muñoz, Manuscript 49

GREAT BRITAIN

British Museum, London

Additional Manuscript, MSS 577

MEXICO

Archivo General de la Nación, Mexico City

Acordada, volumes 9, 31

Bandos, volumes 5, 12, 14, 15, 16, 18

Historia, volumes 72, 74, 578

Real Cédulas (Originales), volumes 107, 109, 110

Tierras, volume 1196

Virreyes, volumes 23, 24, 25, 26, 28

Archivo Histórico de Hacienda, Mexico City

Consulado, legajos 917, 1040

Biblioteca Nacional de México, Mexico City

MSS 432 (1391)

Hemeroteca Nacional de México, Mexico City

Gacetas de México, 1784-1804

UNITED STATES

Arizona State University, Charles Trumbull Hayden Memorial Library

Collection of Eighteenth Century Documents of New Spain, Microfilm Collections

Bancroft Library, Berkeley, California

Mexican Manuscripts, volume 9

Library of Congress, Washington, D.C.

Peter Force Papers
Hans P. Kraus Collection

B. PRINTED DOCUMENTS AND CONTEMPORARY WORKS

Azanza, Miguel José de. Instrucción reservada que dío el Virrey don Miguel José de Azanza a sucesor don Félix Berenquer de Marquina. Prologo y notas de Ernesto de la Torre. México: Editorial Jus, S.A., 1960.

Campillo y Cossío, José. *Nuevo sistema de gobierno económico para la América*. Madrid: Imprenta de J. Ibarra, 1789.

Cavo, Andrés. *Los tres siglos de Méjico durante el gobierno español hasta la entrada del ejército trigarante*. Jalapa: Tipografía de A. Ruíz, 1870.

Croix, Carlos Francisco de. *Instrucción del Virrey Marqués de Croix que deja a su sucesor Antonio María Bucareli*. Prologo y notas de Norman F. Martin. México: Editorial Jus, S.A., 1960.

Flórez Estrada, Álvaro, *Examén imparcial de las disensiones de la América con España de los medios de su reconciliación y de la prosperidad de todas las naciones*. Cádiz: By the Author, 1812.

Gálvez, José de. *Informe general...al excelentísimo senor virrey d. Frey Antonio María Bucareli y Ursua*. México: n.p., 1867.

Hargreaves-Mawdsley, W.N., editor and translator, *Spain under the Bourbons, 1700-1833: A Collection of Documents*. London: Macmillan Company, 1973.

Humboldt, Alejandro de. *Ensayo político sobre el reino de la Nueva España*. ed. Juan A. Ortega y Medina. Mexico: Editorial Porrúa, S.A., 1966.

Humboldt, Alexander von. *Political Essay on the Kingdom of New Spain*. ed. Mary Maples Dunn. New York: Alfred A. Knopf, Inc., 1972.

Lerdo de Tejada, Miguel. *Comercio exterior de México desde la conquista hasta hoy*. Mexico: Impreso por Rafael Rafael, 1853.

Levene, Ricardo, ed. *Documentos para la historia Argentina*. 7 vols. Buenos Aires: Compañía Sud-Americana de Billetes de Banco, 1915-1916.

Longiños Martínez, José. *Journal of José Longiños Martínez: Notes and Observations of the Naturalist of the Botanical Expedition of Old and New California, 1791-1792*. Translated and edited by Lesley Byrd Simpson. San Francisco: John Howell Books, 1961.

O'Crouley, Don Pedro Alonso. *A Description of the Kingdom of New Spain, 1774*. Translated and edited by Sean Galvin. San Francisco: John Howell Books, 1972.

Real ordenanza para el establecimiento e instrucción de intendentes de exército y provincía en el reino de la Nueva España. Madrid: Imprenta de J. Ibarra, 1786.

Revilla Gigedo, segundo conde de, Don Juan Vicente Güemes, Pacheco, Padilla y Horcasitas. Instrucción reservada que el Conde de Revilla Gigedo dío a su sucesor en el mando, Marqués de Branciforte sobre el gobierno de este continente en el tiempo que fué su virrey, 30 de junio de 1794. México: Imprenta por C. Agustín Guiol, 1831.

Veitia Linaje, Joseph de. Norte de la Contratación de las Indias Occidentales. Sevilla: Imprenta de Juan Francisco Blas, 1672.

Velasco Ceballos, Romulo, ed. La administración de D. Frey Antonio María Bucareli y Ursúa. 2 vols. México: Publicaciones del Archivo General de la Nación, 1936.

Ward, Bernardo. Proyecto económico, en que se proponen varias providencías dirigidas a promover los intereses de España, con los medios y fondos necesarios para su plantificación. Madrid: Imprenta de J. Ibarra, 1779.

C. SECONDARY WORKS

Anna, Timothy E. The Fall of the Royal Government in Mexico City. Lincoln: University of Nebraska Press, 1978.

__________. "The Last Viceroys of New Spain and Peru: An Appraisal." American Historical Review 81 (February 1976): 38-65.

__________. "Spain and the Breakdown of the Imperial Ethos: The Problem of Equality." Hispanic American Historical Review 62 (May 1982): 254-272.

__________. Spain and the Loss of America. Lincoln: University of Nebraska Press, 1983.

Archer, Christon I. The Army in Bourbon Mexico, 1760-1810. Albuquerque: University of New Mexico Press, 1977.

__________. "The Army of New Spain and the Wars of Independence." Hispanic American Historical Review 61 (November 1981): 705-714.

Anderson, Bo and Cockcraft, James. "Control and Cooptation in Mexican Politics." International Journal of Comparative Sociology 7 (March 1966): 1-25.

Arcila Farías, Eduardo. Reformas económicas del siglo VIII en Nueva España. 2 vols. México: Sepsententas, 1974.

Arnold, Linda Jo. "Bureaucracy and Bureaucrats in Mexico City: 1742-1835." Ph.D. dissertation, University of Texas, Austin, 1982.

Bakewell, Peter J. Silver Mining and Society in Colonial Mexico: Zacatecas, 1546-1700. Cambridge: Cambridge University Press, 1971.

Bancroft, Hubert H. History of Mexico. 6 vols. San Francisco: A.L. Bancroft and Company, 1883-1888.

Barbier, Jacques A. "The Culmination of the Bourbon Reforms, 1787-1792." Hispanic American Historical Review 57 (February 1977): 51-68.

________________. "Peninsular Finance and Colonial Trade: The Dilemma of Charles IV's Spain." Journal of Latin American Studies 12 (May 1980): 21-37.

Barrett, Ward. The Sugar Hacienda of the Marqueses del Valle. Minneapolis: University of Minnesota Press, 1970.

Bauer, Arnold J. "The Church in the Economy of Spanish America: Censos and Depósitos in the Eighteenth and Nineteenth Centuries." Hispanic American Historical Review 63 (November 1983): 707-734.

Bazant, Jan. "Evolución de la industría textil poblana, 1544-1845." Historia mexicana 13 (abril-junio 1964): 473-516.

Benson, Nettie L., ed. Mexico and the Spanish Cortes, 1810-1822. Austin: University of Texas Press, 1966.

Bitar Letayf, Marcelo. Economistas españoles del siglo XVIII. Madrid: Ediciones Cultura Hispanica, 1968.

Bobb, Bernard E. The Viceregency of Antonio María Bucareli in New Spain, 1771-1779. Austin: University of Texas Press, 1962.

Borah, Woodrow. Silk Raising in Colonial Mexico. Ibero-Americana, vol. 20. Berkeley: University of California Press, 1943.

Boyer, Richard. "Mexico in the Seventeenth Century: Transition of a Colonial Society." Hispanic American Historical Review 57 (August 1977): 455-478.

Brading, David A. "Los españoles en México hacía 1792." Historia mexicana 21 (julio-septiembre 1973): 126-144.

______________. "La estructura de la producción agrícola en el Bajío de 1700 a 1850." Historia mexicana 23 (octubre-diciembre 1973): 197-237.

______________. "Mexican Silver-Mining in the Eighteenth Century: The Revival of Zacatecas." Hispanic American Historical Review 50 (November 1970): 665-681.

______________. Haciendas and Ranchos in the Mexican Bajio: Leon, 1700-1860. Cambridge: Cambridge University Press, 1978.

______________. Miners and Merchants in Bourbon Mexico, 1763-1810. Cambridge: Cambridge University Press, 1971.

Braudel, Fernand. The Wheels of Commerce: Civilization and Capitalism, 15th-18th Century. New York: Harper and Row, Inc., 1982.

Calderón Quijano, José Antonio. "El banco de San Carlos y las comunidades de indios de Nueva España." Anuario de estudios americanos 18 (1962): 1-144.

______________________________. "Ingenieros militares en Nueva España." Anuario de estudios americanos 6 (1949): 1-72.

Callahan, William J. "The Crown and the Promotion of Industry in Eighteenth-Century Spain." Ph.D. dissertation, Harvard University, 1964.

Camp, Roderic A. Mexico's Leaders: Their Education and Recruitment. Tucson: University of Arizona Press, 1980.

Carrera Stampa, Manuel. "The Evolution of Weights and Measures in New Spain." Hispanic American Historical Review 29 (February 1949): 2-24.

__________________________. "Las ferías novohispanas." Historia mexicana 7 (enero-marzo 1953): 319-342.

Chapman, Charles E. A History of Spain. New York: Macmillan Company, 1918.

Cooper, Donald B. Epidemic Disease in Mexico City, 1761-1813: An Administrative, Social, and Medical Study. Austin: University of Texas Press, 1965.

Couturier, Edith B. "Hacienda de Hueyapan: The History of a Mexican Social and Economic Institution, 1550-1940." Ph.D. dissertation, Columbia University, 1965.

Cuenca, Javier Esteban. "Statistics of Spain's Colonial Trade, 1792-1820: Consular Duties, Cargo Inventories, and Balances of Trade." Hispanic American Historical Review 61 (August 1981): 381-428.

Cumberland, Charles C. Mexican Revolution: The Constitutionalist Years. Austin: University of Texas Press, 1972.

__________________. Mexican Revolution: Genesis Under Madero. Austin: University of Texas Press, 1952.

Cutter, Donald C. Malaspina in California. San Francisco: John Howell Books, 1960.

Elliot, John H. Imperial Spain, 1469-1716. New York: St. Martin's Press, 1963.

Felix, David. "Income Inequality in Mexico." Current History 72 (March 1977): 111-114.

Fireman, Janet R. The Spanish Royal Corps of Engineers in the Western Borderlands: Instrument of Bourbon Reform, 1764 to 1815. Glendale, California: Arthur H. Clark Company, 1977.

Fisher, John R. "Imperial 'Free Trade' and the Hispanic Economy, 1778-1796." Journal of Latin American Studies 13 (May 1981): 21-56.

Florescano, Enrique. Precios de maíz y crísis agrícola en México, 1708-1800. México: El Colegio de Mexico, 1969.

Fox, John S. "Antonio de San José Muro: Political Economist of New Spain." Hispanic American Historical Review 21 (August 1941): 410-416.

Fox-Genovese, Elizabeth. The Origins of the Physiocracy. Ithaca: Cornell University Press, 1976.

García Morales, Silvia. "Precios y producción en San Miguel el Grande." Ph.D. dissertation, Universidad Nacional Autónoma de México, 1975.

Garner, Richard L. "Zacatecas, 1750-1821: The Study of a Late Colonial Mexican City." Ph.D. dissertation, University of Michigan, 1970.

Gibson, Charles. The Aztecs Under Spanish Rule: A History of the Indians of the Valley of Mexico, 1519-1810. Stanford: Stanford University Press, 1964.

_______________. Spain in America. New York: Harper and Row, Inc., 1966.

Gónzalez Rodríguez, Miguel A. "La politización: desarrollo político." Pensamiento político 35 (marzo 1972): 357-368.

Greenleaf, Richard E. "The Obraje in the Late Mexican Colony." The Americas 23 (January 1967): 227-250.

Guice, Clarence N. "The Consulado of New Spain, 1595-1795." Ph.D. dissertation, University of California, Berkeley, 1952.

Guthrie, Chester L. "Colonial Economy, Trade, Industry, and Labor in Seventeenth Century Mexico City." Revista de historia de America 7 (diciembre 1939): 103-134.

Hamill, Hugh M. The Hidalgo Revolt: Prelude to Mexican Independence. Gainesville: University of Florida Press, 1966.

Hamnett, Brian R. "Dye Production, Food Supply, and the Laboring Population of Oaxaca, 1750-1820." Hispanic American Historical Review 51 (February 1971): 51-78.

_______________. Politics and Trade in Southern Mexico, 1750-1821. Cambridge: Cambridge University Press, 1971.

Haring, Clarence H. The Spanish Empire in America. New York: Harcourt, Brace, and World, Inc., 1963.

_______________. Trade and Navigation between Spain and the Indies in the Time of the Hapsburgs. Cambridge: Harvard University Press, 1918.

Harris, Charles H. A Mexican Family Empire: The Latifundio of the Sanchez Navarros, 1765-1867. Austin: University of Texas Press, 1975.

Herr, Richard. The Eighteenth Century Revolution in Spain. Princeton: Princeton University Press, 1958.

Hoberman, Louisa S. "Bureaucracy and Disaster: Mexico City and the Flood of 1629." Journal of Latin American Studies 6 (November 1974): 479-230.

________________. "Merchants in Seventeenth-Century Mexico City: A Preliminary Portrait." Hispanic American Historical Review 57 (August 1977): 479-503.

Huntington, Samuel P. Political Order in Changing Societies. New Haven: Yale University Press, 1970.

Johnson, Kenneth F. Mexican Democracy: A Critical View. New York: Praeger Publishers, 1968.

Kagan, Sam. "Penal Servitude in New Spain: The Colonial Textile Industry." Ph.D. dissertation, City University of New York, 1976.

Kicza, John E. Colonial Entrepreneurs: Families and Business in Bourbon Mexico City. Albuquerque: University of New Mexico Press, 1983.

Ladd, Doris M. The Mexican Nobility at Independence, 1780-1826. Austin: University of Texas Press, 1976.

La Force, James C. Development of the Spanish Textile Industry, 1750-1800. Berkeley: University of California Press, 1965.

Lavrin, Asunción. "The Role of the Nunneries in the Economy of New Spain in the Eighteenth Century." Hispanic American Historical Review 46 (November 1966): 371-393.

Leiby, John S. Report to the King: Colonel Juan Camargo y Cavallero's Historical Account of New Spain, 1815. New York: Peter Lang Publishing, Inc., 1984.

Lindley, David B. Haciendas and Economic Development: Guadalajara, Mexico at Independence. Austin: University of Texas Press, 1983.

Lockhart, James and Schwartz, Stuart B. Early Latin America: A History of Colonial Spanish America and Brazil. Cambridge: Cambridge University Press, 1983.

López Escutía, Luís A. "Ideología de las instituciones políticas mexicanas." Pensamiento político 66 (octubre 1974): 165-166.

Lynch, John. Spain Under the Hapsburgs. 2 vols. New York: Oxford University Press, 1964-1969.

____________. Spanish Colonial Administration, 1782-1810: The Intendant System in the Viceroyalty of the Rio de la Plata. London: Clarendon Press, 1958.

MacLachlan, Colin M. Criminal Justice in Eighteenth Century Mexico: A Study of the Tribunal of the Acordada. Berkeley: University of California Press, 1974.

__________ and Rodríguez O., Jaime E. The Forging of the Cosmic Race: A Reinterpretation of Colonial Mexico. Berkeley: University of California Press, 1980.

Manfredini, James M. "The Political Role of the Count of Revillagigedo, Viceroy of New Spain, 1789-1794." Ph.D. dissertation, University of Texas, Austin, 1952.

McAlister, Lyle N. "Social Structure and Social Change in New Spain." Hispanic American Historical Review 43 (August 1963): 349-370.

Meyer, Michael C. and Sherman, William L. The Course of Mexican History. 2 ed. New York: Oxford University Press, 1983.

Moorhead, Max L. New Mexico's Royal Road: Trade and Travel on the Chihuahua Trail. Norman: University of Oklahoma Press, 1958.

Moreno, Frank J. "The Spanish Colonial System: A Functional Approach." Western Political Quarterly 20 (1967): 308-320.

Navarro García, Luís. Don José de Gálvez y la Comandancía General de las Provincias Internas del norte de Nueva España. Sevilla: Escuela de Estudios Hispano-Americanos, 1964.

__________. Intendencias de Indias. Sevilla: Escuela de Estudios Hispano-Americanos, 1959.

Needleman, Martin. "Who Rules Mexico? A Critique of Some Current Views on the Mexican Political Process." Journal of Politics 31 (November 1969): 1011-1034.

Niemeyer Jr., E.V. Revolution at Querétaro: The Mexican Constitutional Convention of 1916-1917. Austin: University of Texas Press, 1974.

Osborn, Wayne S. "Indian Land Retention in Colonial Metztitlán." Hispanic American Historical Review 53 (May 1973): 217-238.

Parry, John H. The Sale of Public Office in the Spanish Indies Under the Hapsburgs. Berkeley: University of California Press, 1953.

_______. The Spanish Seaborne Empire. New York: Alfred A. Knopf, Inc., 1966.

Pérez Verdía, Luís. Historia particular del estado de Jalisco: desde los primeros tiempos de que hay noticía hasta nuestros días. 2 ed. 3 vols. Guadalajara:Gráfica, 1952.

Powell, Philip W. Mexico's Miguel Caldera: The Taming of America's First Frontier, 1548-1597. Tucson: University of Arizona Press, 1977.

_______. Soldiers, Indians, and Silver: North America's First Frontier War. Berkeley: University of California Press, 1952; reprint ed., Tempe: Arizona State University, Center for Latin American Studies, 1975.

Priestley, Herbert I. José de Gálvez, Visitor-General of New Spain, 1765-1771. Berkeley: University of California Press, 1916.

Real Díaz, José Joaquín. "Las ferías de Jalapa." Anuario de estúdios americanos 16 (1959): 167-314.

Renate Moreno, Christiana. Kaufmannschaft und Handelskapitalismus in der Stadt Mexiko, 1759-1778. Bonn: Rheinische Friedrich-Wilhelms-Universität, 1978.

Reyna, José Luís. "Redefining the Authoritarian Regime" in Authoritarianism in Mexico. Philadelphia: Institute for the Study of Human Issues, 1977.

Riley, James D. "The Management of the Estates of the Jesuit Colegio Maxímo de San Pedro y San Pablo in Mexico City." Ph.D. dissertation, Tulane University, 1972.

Ringrose, David R. "Carting in the Hispanic World: An Example of Divergent Development." Hispanic American Historical Review 50 (February 1970): 30-51.

_______. Madrid and the Spanish Economy, 1560-1850. Berkeley: University of California Press, 1983.

Rippy, Merril. "The Economic Repercussions of Expropriation: Case Study, Mexican Oil." Inter-American Economic Affairs 5 (1951): 52-70.

Rivera Cambas, Manuel. Los gobernantes de México. 6 vols. México: Imprenta de J.M. Aguilar, 1872; reprint ed., México: Editorial Citlaltepetl, 1964.

Ross, Stanley R. Francisco I. Madero: Apostle of Mexican Democracy. New York: Columbia University, 1955.

Ruíz, Rámon Eduardo. Mexico: The Challenge of Poverty and Illiteracy. San Marino: Huntington Library, 1963.

Salmoral, Manuel Lucena. "La Memoria de Basadre de 1818 sobre el comercio y contrabando en el Caribe." Jahrbuch für Geschichte von Staat, Wirtschaft und Lateinamerikas 18 (1982): 223-237.

Sarfatti, Magali. Spanish Bureaucratic-Patrimonialism in America. Berkeley and Los Angeles: Institute of International Studies, 1966.

Schurz, William L. The Manila Galleon. New York: E.P. Dutton and Company, 1939.

Serrera Contreras, Rámon María. "La ciudad de Santiago de Querétaro a fines del siglo XVIII: Apuntes para la historia urbana." Anuario de estudios Americanos 30 (1973): 489-555.

________________. Cultivo y manufactura de lino y cañamo en Nueva España, 1777-1800. Sevilla: Escuela de Estudios Hispano-Americanos, 1974.

Smith, Peter H. Labyrinths of Power: Political Recruitment in Twentieth-Century Mexico. Princeton: Princeton University Press, 1979.

Smith, Robert S. "The Institution of the Consulado in New Spain." Hispanic American Historical Review 24 (February 1944): 61-83.

__________. "Sales Taxes in New Spain, 1575-1770." Hispanic American Historical Review 28 (February 1948): 2-37.

__________. "Shipping in the Port of Veracruz, 1790-1821." Hispanic American Historical Review 23 (February 1943): 5-20.

Stein, Stanley J. "Bureaucracy and Business in the Spanish Empire, 1759-1804: Failure of a Bourbon Reform in Mexico and Peru." Hispanic American Historical Review 61 (February 1981): 2-28.

Super, John C. "Queretaro Obrajes: Industry and Trade in Provincial Mexico, 1600-1800." Hispanic American Historical Review 56 (May 1976): 197-216.

Swan, Susan L. "Climate, Crops,and Livestock: Some Aspects of Colonial Mexican Agriculture." Ph.D. dissertation, Washington State University, 1977.

Tardiff, Guillemo. Historia general del comercio exterior mexicano. 2 vols. México: By the Author, 1968.

Taylor, William B. Drinking, Homicide, and Rebellion in Colonial Mexican Villages. Stanford: Stanford University Press, 1979.

________. Landlord and Peasant in Colonial Oaxaca. Stanford: Stanford University Press, 1972.

TePaske, John J. and Klein, Herbert S. "The Seventeehth Century Crisis in New Spain: Myth and Reality?" Past and Present 90 (1981): 116-135.

Thurman, Michael E. The Naval Department of San Blas: New Spain's Bastion for Alta California and Nootka, 1767-1798. Glendale, California: Arthur H. Clark Company, 1967.

Timmons, Wilbert H. Morelos of Mexico: Priest, Soldier, Statesman. El Paso: Texas Western Press, 1963.

Townsend, William C. Lázaro Cárdenas: Mexican Democrat. Ann Arbor: George Wahr Publishing Co., 1952.

Tútino, John M. "Creole Mexico: Spanish Elites, Haciendas, and Indian Towns, 1750-1810." Ph.D. dissertation, University of Texas, Austin, 1976.

Vanderwood, Paul J. Disorder and Progress: Bandits, Police, and Mexican Development. Lincoln: University of Nebraska Press, 1981.

________. "Mexico's Rurales: Image of a Society in Transition." Hispanic American Historical Review 61

Van Young, Eric. Hacienda and Market in Eighteenth Century Mexico: The Rural Economy of the Guadalajara Region, 1675-1820. Berkeley: University of California Press, 1981.

Walker, Geoffrey J. Spanish Politics and Imperial Trade, 1700-1789. Bloomington: Indiana University Press, 1979.

Wilkie, James W. The Mexican Revolution: Federal Expenditure and Social Change Since 1910. Berkeley: University of California Press, 1967.

Zabala y Lera, Pío. España bajo los Borbones. Barcelona: Editorial Labor, S.A., 1955.

John S. Leiby

Report to the King

Colonel Juan Camargo y Cavallero's Historical Account of New Spain, 1815.

American University Studies: Series IX, History, Vol. 3.
ISBN 0-8204-0050-5 225 pp. pb./lam. US $ 22.70

recommended prices - alterations reserved

Colonel Juan Camargo y Cavallero's chronicle stands as testament to the grandeur of late Bourbon Mexico. This report was written in 1815 in the midst of the Mexican Wars of Independence. This member of the Spanish Royal Corps of Engineers provides firsthand information on the political, economic, and military conditions existing during this turbulent phase of Mexican history. Camargo's chronicle is consequently a major source about the effects of the early nineteenth century insurrections.

Contents: The book describes the social, political, economic, and military conditions existing during the Mexican Wars of Independence.

PETER LANG PUBLISHING, INC.
62 West 45th Street
USA - New York, NY 10036

Judith Gentleman

Mexican Oil and Dependent Developement

American University Studies: Series X, Political Science. Vol. 2.
ISBN 0-8204-0063-7 270 pp. hardcover/lam. US $ 29.–

recommended prices - alterations reserved

This study examines Mexico's experience in the development of its vast hydrocarbon resources during the latter half of the 1970s and early 1980s. The study assesses the impact that Mexico's dependent state status has upon the development of the resource and explores the question of whether the oil boom provoked a greater internatilization of the Mexican economy or led to a favorable redefination of the terms of Mexico's dependence. The study examines the impact of development of the resource upon the state capitalist model and considers the viability of that model in the current context.

Contents: A study of the impact of petroleum development upon Mexico in the late 1970's and early 1980s–Assesses the effect upon Mexico's dependent state status and upon the state capitalist model of development.

PETER LANG PUBLISHING, INC.
62 West 45th Street
USA - New York, NY 10036